Study and Revise

GCSE

Modern World History

John Patrick

Key to Symbols

As you read through this book you will notice the following symbols. They will help you find your way around the book more quickly.

 (a) Notes, Tips

(b) Check boxes

 Specimen questions

 Model answers

 Hints

Copyright © John Patrick 1997, 2004 extra material © Christopher Culpin 2004

First published in this edition 2004
Exclusively for WHSmith by
Hodder Murray
338 Euston Road
London NW1 3BH

Impression number   10 9 8 7 6 5 4 3 2 1
Year   2010 2009 2008 2007 2006 2005 2004

Illustrations: Harvey Collins, Andrea Norton, Stephen Ramsay, Oxford Designers & Illustrators

Printed and bound in the UK by Scotprint

A CIP record for this book is available from the British Library

ISBN 0 340 858664

Contents

Introduction

This book is designed to help you achieve a better grade in GCSE Modern World History.

Topics

Before starting your revision, you should get a list of the topics you need to know from your teacher, together with a note of which ones are examined in Paper One and which in Paper Two.

This book covers all, or nearly all, of the topics you have to know. Different examination courses have different options, so you will find that you do not have to do all the topics in this book.

In each chapter

Preview

Each chapter starts with a 'preview' – a list of the key things you need to know in that chapter. Start by checking your own knowledge. Then read the chapter, looking for help on any gaps you have found in your understanding. Then check yourself again. The preview can also be a useful 'night before the exam' checklist.

Sources

Every History examination has a number of sources, which you have to read and understand. So a major part of every chapter of this book consists of historical sources – letters, speeches, cartoons, photographs, posters, diaries, memoirs, oral evidence.

Each source has been given its *provenance* – who made it and when. These have been kept simple, as they are in the exam, but as you read and study the source, think about how the provenance affects how you use it.

Dates and timelines

There are lists of dates and timelines in each chapter to help you get the important chronology straight.

Notes

Some sections of the text are displayed as 'Notes' to draw your attention to specific points, features on maps, or statistics. These are laid out clearly, to help you with revision.

Specimen questions

Throughout the book there are specimen questions in just the same wording as the real questions in the examination. Some test your understanding of the history, some ask you to go more deeply into evaluating the sources.

The number of marks usually awarded is shown. Use these marks as clues to how much to write in your answer: 5–7 marks means a paragraph; 8-10 marks means about a page; 11–12 marks means a short essay, and so on.

Hints

Hints are provided for many of the specimen questions to guide you. They suggest angles for an answer which you might not have thought of.

Tips

These give you advice on how to tackle your learning and revision.

Model answers

Several model answers are given. Look at these carefully: how long are they? How do they start and finish? How is the answer divided up? In what order are the various parts of an answer dealt with?

Check boxes

Each section ends with a revision tip, or brief reminder of what you need to know or be able to do.

Some milestones in twentieth-century history

1903	WSPU (Suffragettes) founded
1905	Russian Revolution
1911	National Insurance Act passed
1914	First World War begins
1917	Russian Revolution – Lenin comes to power
1918	First World War ends
1919	Peace treaties signed
	League of Nations established
1922	Mussolini seizes power in Italy
1923	Collapse of the German mark
1924	Death of Lenin – Stalin takes over in USSR
1928	Votes for all women in Britain
1929	Wall Street Crash
1931	Japan invades Manchuria
1932	Depth of the Great Depression
1933	Hitler takes over in Germany
	Roosevelt becomes President of USA – launches 'New Deal'
1935	Mussolini invades Abyssinia
1937	Civil War breaks out in Spain
1939	Second World War begins
1941	Pearl Harbor – Japan and USA enter war
1945	A-bombs dropped on Japan
	Second World War ends
	United Nations Organisation established
1947	India and Pakistan granted independence
1948	Berlin blockade
	National Health Service introduced in Britain
1949	Mao sets up People's Republic of China
1950	Korean War breaks out
1953	Death of Stalin
1956	Hungarian revolt
1961	Berlin Wall built
1962	Cuban Missile Crisis
1965	US troops land in Vietnam
1968	The Prague Spring
1975	US troops leave Vietnam
1980	Rise of Solidarity in Poland
1985	Gorbachev takes over in the USSR
1989	Berlin Wall opened

Preview

What you need to know:

- Why war broke out in 1914
- The war in France and Belgium
- The character and ability of Douglas Haig
- Why Allied troops landed at Gallipoli and what happened as a result
- The part played by air forces in the war
- The naval war
- How the war affected life in Britain
- How the war ended

The causes of the war

Underlying causes

Between 1870 and 1914 the new German Empire upset Britain, France and Russia in various ways:

- Germany's trade and industry was booming
- Germany had captured Alsace-Lorraine from France
- Germany's connections with Morocco and Baghdad troubled Russia, France and Britain
- Germany's dreadnoughts threatened Britain.

At the same time, Austria–Hungary was on bad terms with Russia over the Balkans, a collection of newly independent countries. Both Austria and Russia wanted to dominate them.

Treaty timeline

1879 Germany allied with Austria. (In 1913 the German Kaiser told the Austrian government: '*You can be certain I stand behind you, and am ready to draw the sword whenever your action makes it necessary.*')

1891 Russia allied with France. (In 1892 the Tsar of Russia wrote: '*In case of war between France and Germany we must hurl ourselves upon the Germans.*')

1904 Britain allied with France. (In 1906 the British Foreign Minister wrote: '*The British people would not tolerate France's being involved in a war with Germany ... Any English government would be forced to help France.*')

Russia, Germany, Austria, France and Britain all feared that their enemies might attack them. So they made treaties to protect themselves (see map and treaty timeline).

Specimen question

If war broke out in Europe after 1904, which countries would have been bound to fight (a) on Germany's side and (b) against Germany? Explain your answer.   [4 marks]

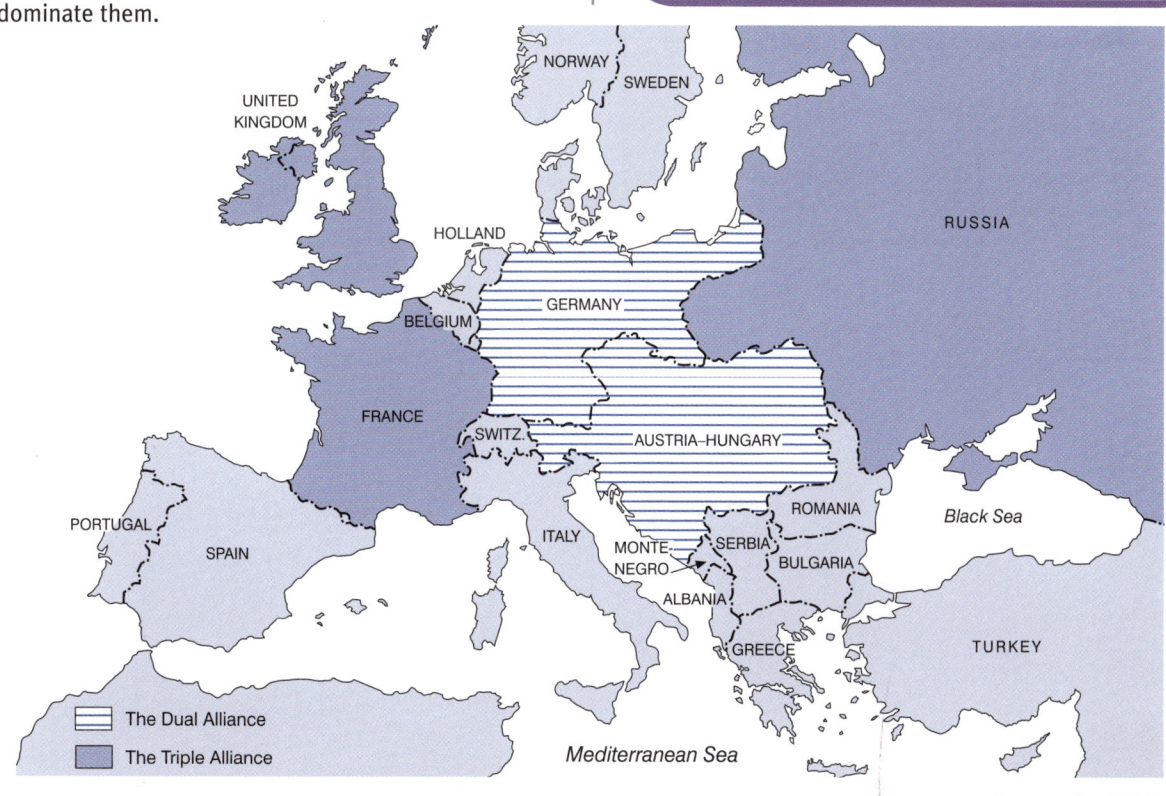

Key:
- The Dual Alliance
- The Triple Alliance

Europe in 1904

The outbreak of war
The Schlieffen Plan

When France and Russia made their alliance it meant that, if there was a war, Germany would have to fight on two fronts. In 1905 Field Marshal Alfred Von Schlieffen worked out a plan to cope with this. The box below and map will remind you of its main features.

The Schlieffen Plan was very risky. It depended on Russia taking a long time to mobilise. It also ignored the fact that Britain had promised (1839) to defend Belgium if she was attacked.

The lead-up to war

None of the governments wanted a large-scale war in 1914. A series of events pushed them into it. The timeline is on the right.

Schlieffen order of events

(**Note:** This is the order in which events were meant to happen.)

1   War breaks out.
2   Russia begins to mobilise.
3   Germany masses troops on the Belgian border.
4   France attacks Germany through Alsace-Lorraine.
5   Germany smashes south through Belgium and cuts off Paris.
6   France surrenders.
7   German troops travel by rail to fight the Russians in the east.

Outbreak of war timeline

28 June	Gavrilo Princip, a Serb, assassinated Archduke Franz Ferdinand. Austria blamed Serbia.
23 July	Austria sent Serbia ten demands. Russia advised Serbia to give way.
25 July	Serbia accepted eight out of ten.
26 July	Austria declared war on Serbia.
30 July	Russia began to mobilise.
31 July	Germany told Russia to stop.
1 August	Russia refused. Germany declared war on Russia.
2 August	Germany declared war on France and asked Belgium for permission to march through.
3 August	Belgium refused and asked for Britain's help.
4 August	Germany marched into Belgium and refused to withdraw. Britain declared war on Germany.

Notes

Remember why these events followed each other:

- Princip assassinated Franz Ferdinand because he wanted Austria to move out of Bosnia and Herzegovina.
- The Austrians attacked Serbia because they wanted to extend Austria's influence in the Balkans.
- Russia mobilised because she wanted to prevent Austria taking over in the Balkans.
- Germany declared war on Russia and France because the Schlieffen Plan depended on Germany defeating France before Russia had time to mobilise.
- Britain declared war because Germany invaded Belgium, which Britain had promised to protect.

Exam tip

The most likely questions about the outbreak of the First World War will concentrate either on why the European powers were on such bad terms after 1900, or on the events leading to war in 1914. To answer the questions below, you need to consider the author of each source, the circumstances under which it was written/spoken and your own knowledge of the situation.

Source A

'Just for a word Britain is going to make war on a kindred nation that asks only friendship. Just for a word: "neutrality"! Just for a scrap of paper!'

German Chancellor speaking to the British ambassador, 4 August 1914

Source B

'I never doubted that, if the Germans interfered with the . . . independence of Belgium, we were in honour bound to discharge our treaty obligations to that country.'

David Lloyd George, British Cabinet Minister in 1914: *War Memoirs* (1933)

Source C

'Which of us cares about Serbia? Which of us wants to see Europe at war because of these savages in the Balkans? There is probably not a single Englishman who wants war under these circumstances.'

Letter in the *Daily Mirror*, 3 August 1914

Source D

'If the German navy ever became superior to ours, the German army can conquer this country.'

Sir Edward Grey, British Foreign Minister: Memo to George V, 1912

Specimen question

1 Study Sources A and B. Are the two sources convincing evidence of what the German and British governments thought about Belgian neutrality in 1914? Explain your answer. **[9 marks]**

Model answer

Source A shows that the German government did not think that the promises made in 1839 to protect Belgium mattered. It was spoken by the head of the German government when face to face with the British ambassador. He seems to have been upset, and what he said seems to show that his government did not take international treaties seriously. He had no motive for saying this if it was not true. So it probably was. Lloyd George's statement (Source B) shows that he and the government took the promises made to Belgium seriously. He wrote it many years later, in a book which he hoped would make people think well of him. So it may not be true. But it fits in with what is known about the British government's attitude from other sources. So it is probably reliable.

Specimen question

2 Does Source C prove that Britain would not have entered the First World War if Germany had withdrawn from Belgium on 4 August 1914? Explain your answer. **[6 marks]**

Model answer

Source C is from a letter to a newspaper. It proves only what the writer of the letter thought. But it does show that some people in Britain were very unwilling to go to war over Austria's treatment of Serbia. But even if Germany had not invaded Belgium, or had withdrawn when threatened by Britain, the British government would still probably have had to go to war because of the Anglo-French treaty of 1904. The source shows that this might have been unpopular with some people. Germany's invasion of Belgium made the declaration of war more popular in Britain than it would have been otherwise.

Specimen question

3 Use your own knowledge of the period and the sources to explain why Britain and Germany were on such bad terms in 1914. [15 marks]

Hints

To get high marks on this question you need to blend together information from the sources with what you already know. Writing out your notes on the topic will not be enough. Remember to concentrate on Germany's relations with <u>Britain</u>. You will get no marks for saying how she annoyed France or Russia. The spider diagram below shows how you might plan your answer.

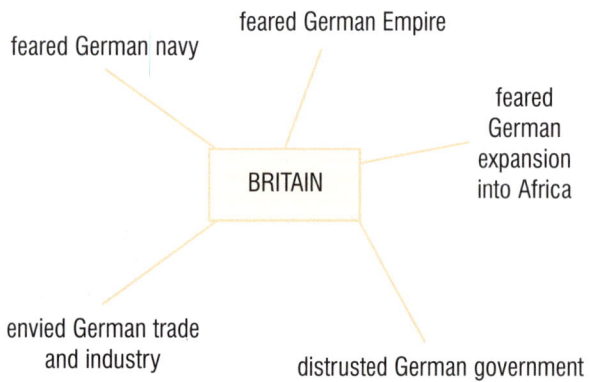

Check

That you understand how and why war broke out in August 1914.

The Western Front

The German attack

When the war began, the Germans put the Schlieffen Plan into effect, but it did not work (*see* map opposite). This was partly because the German High Command did not use as many troops to attack France as Von Schlieffen had planned.

Notes

The map opposite contains a lot of information. It shows how:

1 the Germans drove south from Belgium

2 the French
   (a) moved their army from the Alsace-Lorraine front to block the Germans on the River Marne
   (b) brought out an army from Paris

3 the British forces first fought against the Germans at Mons, and then retreated to link up with the French on the Marne

4 the Allies stopped the German advance at the Battle of the Marne (September 1914).

Tip

Maps can help you to understand and remember. Try drawing your own to help with your revision.

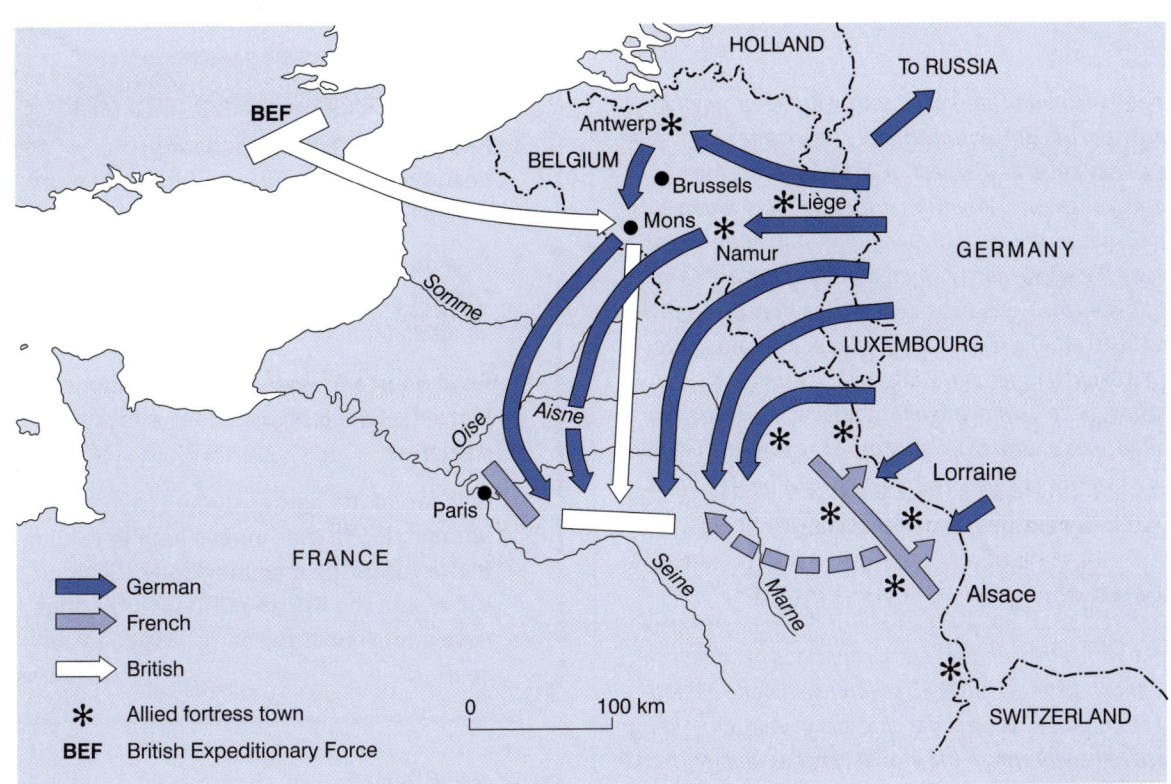

The Western Front

Key:
- → German
- → French
- → British
- ✳ Allied fortress town
- BEF British Expeditionary Force

0 — 100 km

Source

'Our men are done in. For four days they have been marching 40 km a day ... They march with their eyes closed, singing in chorus so that they shall not fall asleep on the march.'

A German officer quoted in John Terraine: *Mons* (1960)

Specimen question

What evidence is there that the speed of the French retreat made things difficult for the Germans? [3 marks]

Trench warfare

After the Battle of the Marne the two opposing armies established lines of trenches stretching from the English Channel to the Swiss frontier. The diagram below will remind you of the main points about trench warfare.

The key features of trench warfare were lines of trenches strongly defended by barbed wire and machine guns. Generals on both sides wanted to break through. Attacks on trenches cost enormous numbers of lives. On the first day of the Battle of the Somme in 1916, 20,000 British troops were killed and 40,000 injured. One battalion lost 497 men out of 730 in one day. Ludendorff described the situation in the trenches in 1917: *'It was no longer life, it was mere unspeakable suffering.'*

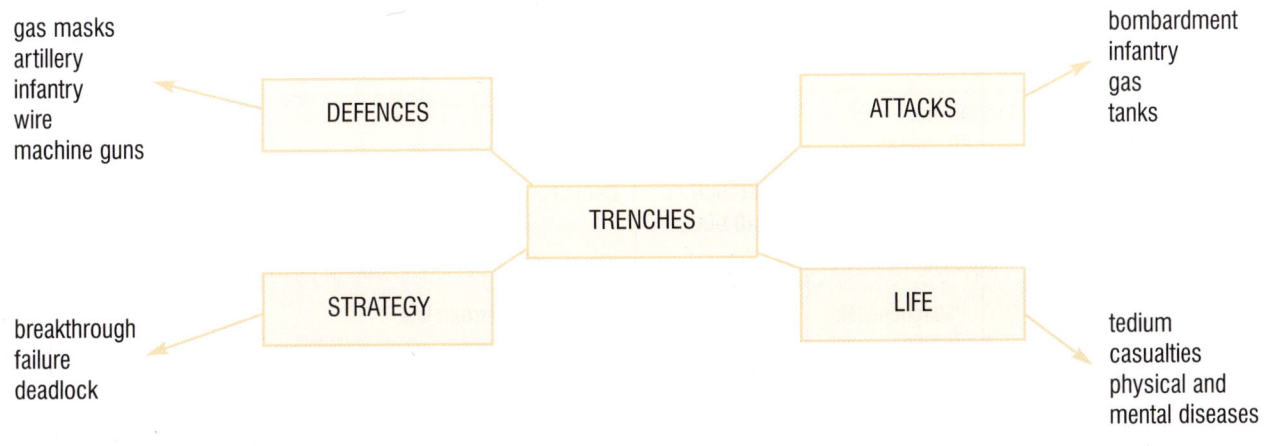

gas masks
artillery
infantry
wire
machine guns

DEFENCES

ATTACKS

bombardment
infantry
gas
tanks

TRENCHES

breakthrough
failure
deadlock

STRATEGY

LIFE

tedium
casualties
physical and
mental diseases

The First World War

Source A

'A series of extended lines of infantry were seen moving forward from the British trenches . . . They came at a steady, easy pace, as if expecting to find nothing alive in our front trenches . . . When the British line was within a hundred metres the rattle of machine gun and rifle broke out along the whole line . . . Immediately afterwards a mass of shells from the German batteries in rear tore through the air and burst among the advancing lines . . . All along the line men could be seen throwing up their arms and collapsing, never to move again . . . Again and again the extended lines of British infantry broke against the German defence like waves against a cliff, only to be beaten back.'

M Gerster: *Die Swaben an der Ancre* (1920)

Source B

'I awoke with a tremendous start, conscious of noise, incessant and almost musical, so intense that it seemed as if a hundred devils were dancing in my brain. Everything seemed to be vibrating – the ground, my dug-out, my bed.'

Arthur Behrend, describing being bombarded

Source C

'The ground between our trench and the ruins beyond was merely a stretch of craters and burnt-out grass broken up by tangled wire, not unlike gorse bushes. The dead were lying there in all conceivable attitudes, rotting in the sun.'

Paul Maze, a French soldier, writing in 1932

Source D

'If you want the old battalion,

We know where they are

They're hanging on the old barbed wire.'

A First World War British army marching song

Specimen questions

1 **Read Source A. What weapons destroyed the infantry's efforts to capture the enemy trenches?** [3 marks]

2 **How does Source B help to justify Ludendorff's description of trench warfare as 'unspeakable suffering'?** [3 marks]

3 **Read Source C. How did the conditions Paul Maze described hinder those attacking the trenches?** [4 marks]

4 **How far do the figures quoted in the introduction to the sources help to explain the words of the marching song (Source D)? Would the British military authorities have approved of the song? Explain your answer.** [6 marks]

New weapons

Two new weapons were tried to break the deadlock:

- **Poison gas**
  This failed because sometimes the wind changed and blew the gas back on the attackers. Also gas masks were developed to neutralise it.

- **Tanks**
  These were used to drive straight over the trenches. Tanks failed because they were slow and unreliable and got stuck in the mud. And even if they broke through, the following infantry still had to face machine guns.

In spite of the lack of success, the attacks continued.

Western Front offensives timeline

Date	Place	Casualties	Comments
1916 (Feb–Jun)	Verdun (German)	F 315,000 G 280,000	Aimed to destroy Verdun and break French army. Failed.
1916 (Jul–Nov)	Somme (Allied)	A 790,000 G 540,000	Dented the German lines slightly.
1917 (April)	Aisne (French)	A 270,000	French driven back; 750,000 of them mutinied.
1917 (Jul–Nov)	Passchendaele (British)	B 500,000 G 270,000	Dented the German line.

Note: The aim of all the offensives, except Verdun, was to break through. Casualty figures (F = French, G = German, A = Allied, B = British) are approximate. Also remember that many soldiers were injured on several occasions and were counted as casualties every time.

Notes

Notice how much information can be crammed into a table. Compile your own tables to help with your revision. Use the table and the sources opposite to find out the following:

1 What happened at Verdun in 1916?

2 When and where did French troops mutiny?

3 What reasons did they have for mutinying?

4 Were the attacks on the Somme and Passchendaele successes or failures? Give reasons for your answers.

Source A

'The story is the same story I have had to tell so many times, the story of an attack pushed with perfect determination and gallantry to final and complete success.'

Report in *The Times*, October 1917

Source B

'Still the guns churned this treacherous slime. Every day conditions grew worse. What had once been difficult now became impossible.'

General Hubert Gough, writing of the October 1917 attack: *The Fifth Army* (1931)

Source C

'Lines of grey, muttering faces, marked with fear,

They leave the trenches, going over the top,

While time ticks blank and busy on their wrists,

And hope, with furtive eyes and grappling fists,

Flounders in mud. O Jesus, make it stop!'

Siegfried Sassoon: *Counter-Attack* (1918)

Source D

No Man's Land in Passchendaele in 1917

Specimen question

1 Sources A and B both describe the Battle of Passchendaele in 1917. To what extent do they contradict each other? Which do you consider is the more reliable? Explain your answer using the other sources and your own knowledge.

[9 marks]

Hints

To show how they contradict each other, compare 'final and complete success' in Source A with 'impossible' in Source B. Source A was written by a journalist. Where did he get his information? Is this likely to be a reliable source? Who were his readers? What did they want to read? Why? Source B was written by a British general many years later. Was he likely to minimise the success of British troops? Which of the two does Source D seem to support? In any case, from your own knowledge, what was the result of the Battle of Passchendaele?

Specimen question

2 Source C is from a poem written by an officer who served in the trenches. What can it tell us about fighting on the Western Front?

[6 marks]

Model answer

Source C is a poem about feelings. It tells us what Sassoon thought people felt when they were going over the top in an attack. It gives the impression that they felt ill, that they were frightened, that time meant nothing to them, and that as they floundered in the mud they lost all hope and prayed for it all to stop. Sassoon had lived in the trenches, and knew what it was like. In any case, the feelings he describes seem reasonable under the circumstances, and fit in with other accounts, so it is probably an accurate account of what many infantrymen felt like when attacking.

Specimen question

3 Using the sources and your own knowledge, explain why trench warfare resulted in years of deadlock.

[12 marks]

Hints

Use all the information mentioned in the section on trench warfare to show how strong trench defences were compared with the forces available to attack them. Use Sources B and D in this section to highlight the effects of bombardments and the limited usefulness of tanks. Source C will show how pointless many of the infantry thought it was to attack. Any system where defence is so much stronger than attack is bound to lead to deadlock. You would get extra credit for pointing out that trench warfare in the American Civil War (1861–65) led to much the same problem. Examiners like you to be able to show how the events you are describing fit in with other times and other places.

Check

That you understand how trench warfare resulted in deadlock.

Douglas Haig

Douglas Haig was the British Commander in Chief. He and his staff played a very important part in deciding how the war should be fought.

Source A

'We have inflicted very heavy losses on the enemy ... In another six weeks the enemy should be hard put to it to find men ... The maintenance of a steady offensive pressure will result eventually in his complete overthrow.'

Douglas Haig: *Diary* (August 1916)

Source B

'I told [a general] that I thought the German was now nearly at his last resources and that there was only <u>one</u> <u>sound</u> plan to follow, viz., <u>without delay</u> to:

1   *Send to France every possible man*

2   *Send to France every possible aeroplane*

3   *Send to France every possible gun.'*

Douglas Haig: *Diary* (June 1917)

Source C

'Blood and mud, blood and mud, they can think of nothing better.'

Lloyd George, British Prime Minister, speaking of British generals in September 1917

Source D

'Unfortunately Haig placed complete confidence in General Charteris, head of his Intelligence Service … Charteris always told Haig something he especially wanted to hear: … that there were no Germans on our front, or that they were … exhausted. These misconceptions … cost the British army dearly.'

General Hubert Gough: *Soldiering On* (1954)

Specimen question

1   **Haig was accused of being too optimistic, obstinate and unimaginative. How far do Sources A, B and C support this accusation?**   **[6 marks]**

Hint

Remember when the war, in fact, ended. Was Haig's view in 1916 and 1917 optimistic? Remember the Battle of the Somme in 1916. Was it obstinate of Haig to want more resources in France in 1917? Lloyd George clearly thought Haig and the other generals were unimaginative. But what alternatives to 'blood and mud' were there?

Specimen question

2   **How far does Source D (a) explain and (b) excuse Haig's optimism?**   **[4 marks]**

Check

What do you think of Douglas Haig? Can you defend your view?

Gallipoli

At the end of 1914 the Russians asked Britain to help in the war against Turkey. The government decided to attack the Dardanelles. Winston Churchill, who helped to organise the attack, thought it would be better *'than sending our armies to chew barbed wire in Flanders'*.

In all, the Gallipoli campaign cost the Allies more than 200,000 dead, sick and wounded, and a huge amount of ammunition and supplies. It gained nothing.

Specimen question

The Gallipoli campaign made it easier for Haig to argue that all available forces should be sent to France. Why was this?

[4 marks]

Gallipoli timeline

March 1915	Naval attack on Dardanelles. Then Turks strengthened defences.
April 1915	Allied troops landed on five Cape Helles beaches and Anzac Cove. Failed to advance inland.
August 1915	Allied troops landed at Suvla Bay. Failed to advance inland.
December 1915	Troops withdrawn from Anzac and Suvla.
January 1916	Troops withdrawn from Helles.

Check

That you understand what happened at Gallipoli, and what the results were.

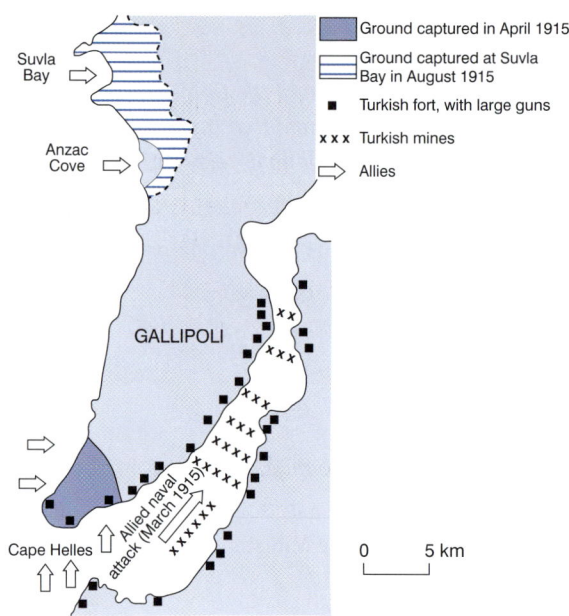

Ground captured in April 1915
Ground captured at Suvla Bay in August 1915
■ Turkish fort, with large guns
x x x Turkish mines
⇨ Allies

The Gallipoli campaign

The air war

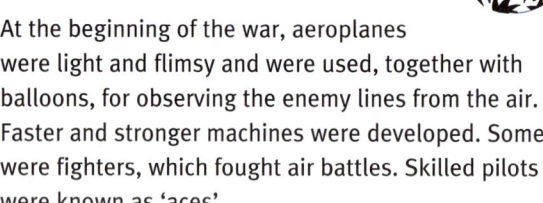

Notes

At the beginning of the war, aeroplanes were light and flimsy and were used, together with balloons, for observing the enemy lines from the air. Faster and stronger machines were developed. Some were fighters, which fought air battles. Skilled pilots were known as 'aces'.

At the beginning of the war, Germany possessed a number of airships called Zeppelins which bombed British towns, causing damage and casualties. Later in the war aeroplanes were powerful enough to carry bombs, and both Britain and Germany used them to raid enemy territory.

But war in the air played only a small part in the First World War.

Check

That you understand developments in the air war.

The war at sea

Notes

Before the war, Germany and Britain both spent huge sums of money on Dreadnought battleships which were expected to play an important part in the war. But, partly because they were so expensive, Dreadnoughts spent most of the war in harbour. The most important part in the war at sea was played by submarines.

Specimen questions

Use the timeline on page 11 to answer the following questions:

1 Both Germany and Britain claimed to have won the Battle of Jutland. How could that be?   [6 marks]

2 The German navy took a great risk in 1917, which did not come off. Explain.   [6 marks]

Check

That you understand the part played by the navies in the war.

Navy timeline

1914	British	Blockaded Germany throughout the war.
	British	Falklands: Sank German ships trying to return from the Pacific.
1915	German	Ultimatum that U-boats would, without warning, sink ships approaching Britain. Sank *Lusitania*, killing 128 Americans. Germans withdrew warning.
1916	German	Fleet put to sea. So did British. Battle of Jutland. British lost more ships, but Germans went back to port and stayed there.
1917	German	New U-boat warning. Sank ships (including US) on way to Britain. At first very successful.
	British	Organised ships into convoys. Cut losses.
	USA	Declared war on Germany.

The Home Front

Before the war broke out in 1914, Sir Edward Grey said, *'If we are engaged in a war we shall suffer but little more than we shall suffer if we stand aside.'* In fact the war hit Britain hard, and brought about many changes. *See* also pages 118–122.

Source A

1918 WRAF recruiting poster

Notes

- **Bureaucracy**
  A J P Taylor, the historian, wrote that *'until 1914 a sensible, law-abiding Englishman could pass through life and hardly notice the existence of the state, beyond the post office and the policeman.'* By the end of the war, the state was interfering in everyday lives in all areas.

- **Morals**
  The horrors of war made many people lose their faith in God. The uncertainty of life, particularly for soldiers, led some young people to enjoy sex as often as possible while they could.

- **Class**
  Social classes mingled more in the war than ever before, in hospitals, factories and in the trenches. This helped to break down rigid class barriers.

- **Women**
  Four million young men joined the forces during the war and had to be replaced in the workforce. The number of women working in trade and industry increased by over a million. Their work was essential, and helped to win them respect and the vote. In addition their pay made them more independent.

- **Casualties**
  Combined casualties from bombardments and air raids were 1550 killed and 4733 wounded.

- **Shortages**
  The U-boat war, especially in 1917, led to shortages of some sorts of food, which were rationed in 1918. There were also shortages of coal and coke.

'In this war [women] have invaded the spheres hitherto considered sacred to men . . . and they have done all these things with an efficiency which has surprised and delighted the whole nation.'

Neville Chamberlain, Director of National Service: Speech, 1917

'By the end of the war, it was no longer true that a woman's place was in the home.'

A J P Taylor: *The First World War* (1963)

Specimen question

1   Study Sources A and B. To what extent do they show that women's work and people's opinions about them changed in the war? Explain your answer.   [9 marks]

Model answer

Before the war, the idea of a woman joining a branch of the fighting services would have seemed very strange. On the other hand, the poster (Source A) emphasises posts as clerks, waitresses and cooks, all jobs that women might have done before the war. But they would not have been employed as motor cyclists. Neville Chamberlain's speech (Source B) shows that by 1917 women had taken over men's jobs in civilian life and done them well. But he was 'surprised and delighted' that they had been able to do this. So before the war he must have had a low opinion of women's abilities. So the two sources show that during the war women joined the forces, did work hitherto only done by men and that as a result people had a higher opinion of them than before.

Specimen question

2   Using the sources and your own knowledge, explain briefly what women did during the war to justify A J P Taylor's claim. To what extent was the claim still true after the war?   [12 marks]

Hints

Notice that you are asked to 'explain' what women did during the war, not to list their contributions. So you need to think carefully how to present all the information briefly. How about the following points?

1   Was it ever true that 'a woman's place was in the home'? What about textile workers and elementary teachers?

2   But many more women took work outside the home during the war.

3   Some did jobs created by the war – for example in the forces (Source A) and munitions factories.

4   Some replaced the men who had gone into the forces. This involved lots of different jobs. You would not be expected to give more than a few examples.

5   At the end of the war the men wanted their jobs back and the wartime jobs disappeared.

6   As a result many women lost their jobs and went back to their 'places' in the home. But they got the vote, which showed that it was recognised that they had some interests outside the home.

Check

That you understand how the war changed life in Britain.

The end of the war

Two events in 1917 broke the deadlock and ended the war. The USA declared war on Germany, and the new revolutionary government in Russia made peace with Germany. Ludendorff decided to use the German troops who had been fighting in Russia to attack and defeat the French and British armies in France before the Americans could come and help them. Ludendorff attacked in March 1918. The map on page 13 will remind you of what happened. Notice how, for the first time since 1914, the Germans broke through. Then in August, the Allies counter-attacked and drove them back.

Also, there were strikes in Germany and the navy mutinied. In November the German government surrendered.

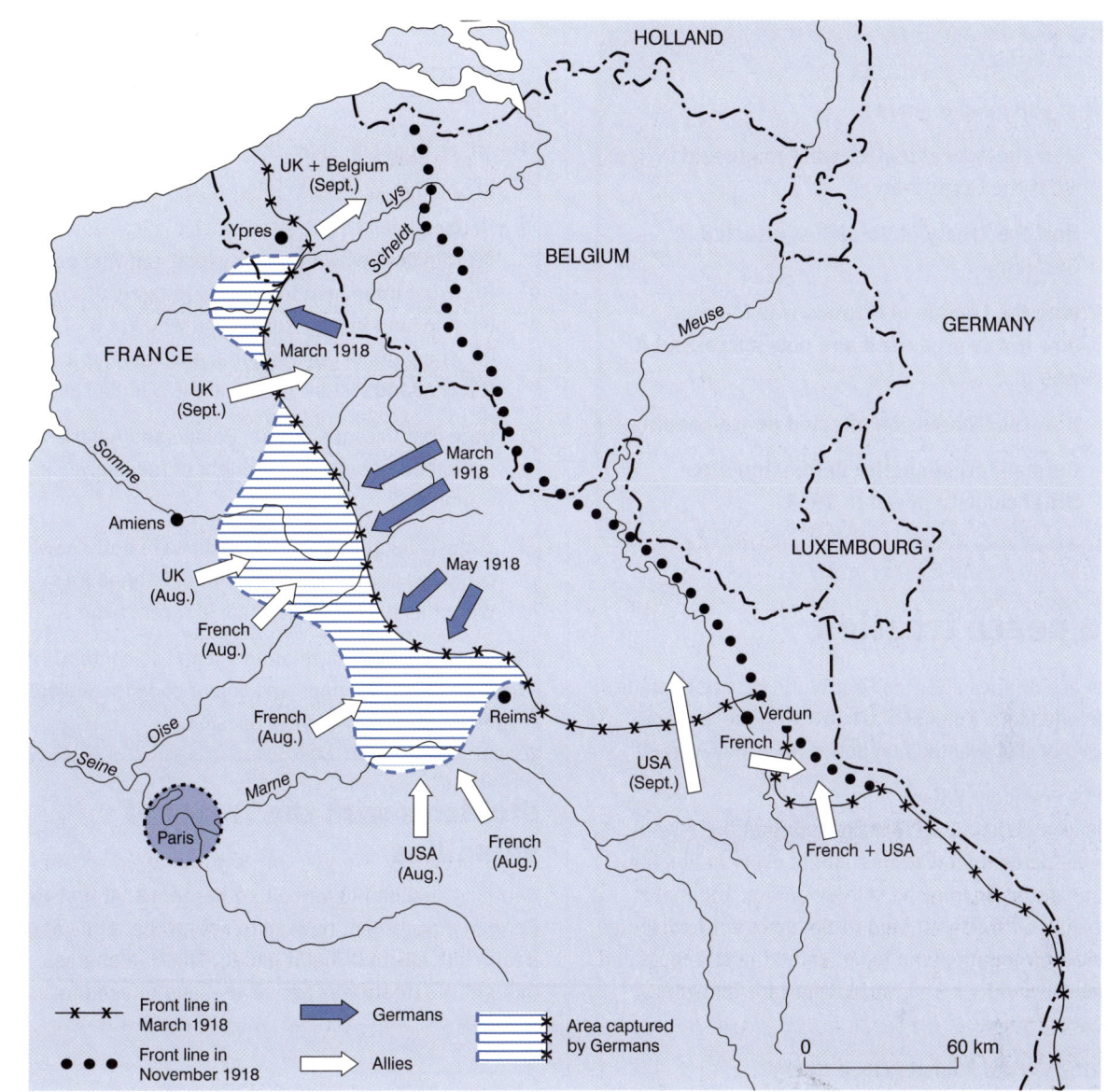

The front line in 1918

'Our troops are exhausted and their numbers have dwindled terribly ... They surrender in hordes whenever the enemy attacks. Whatever happens we must obtain peace, before the enemy breaks through into Germany.'

Crown Prince Rupprecht of Bavaria, a German General: Report, 18 October 1918

Source B

'The war was now lost ... After the way in which our troops on the western front had been used up, we had to count on being driven back again and again. Our situation could only get worse, never better.'

General Ludendorff's evidence to a post-war Reichstag committee

Specimen question

After the war, many Germans, including Hitler, said that the German army had not been defeated, but had been 'stabbed in the back' by the politicians who had surrendered unnecessarily. Does Prince Rupprecht's report prove Hitler wrong? Explain your answer. **[6 marks]**

Check

That you understand why the war ended in 1918.

The peace treaties

The peace treaties after the First World War were made by three leaders. You need to know who the leaders were, what they wanted and how strong they were:

- **USA President Wilson**
  He wanted above all to make sure that there would never be another war. He thought every nation had the right to be free and self-governing, and that a League of Nations should be set up to settle disputes between countries. He represented the strongest and richest country in the world. This gave him great power.

- **British Prime Minister Lloyd George**
  He wanted a just peace. He said, *'We must not allow any sense of revenge, any grasping desire to override the spirit of righteousness.'* But his power depended on British MPs. Most of them wanted Germany to be punished.

- **French Prime Minister Clemençeau**
  Clemençeau, supported by the majority of the French, wanted to regain Alsace-Lorraine and to weaken Germany so that it would never again be able to attack France.

Five treaties were signed at the end of the war:

- Treaty of Versailles, 1919 – dealt with Germany
- Treaty of St Germain, 1919 – dealt with Austria
- Treaty of Neuilly, 1919 – dealt with Bulgaria
- Treaty of Trianon, 1920 – dealt with Hungary
- Treaty of Sèvres 1920 – dealt with Turkey.

Germany was not allowed to take part in the negotiations.

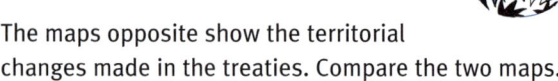

Notes

The maps opposite show the territorial changes made in the treaties. Compare the two maps.

1 Notice:
   (a) the land which Germany lost, and who got it
   (b) what happened to Austria–Hungary
   (c) the land lost by Russia and who got it
   (d) the land lost by Bulgaria, and who got it
   (e) the land lost by Turkey in the Middle East.

2 Note that Czechoslovakia, Poland and Austria all contained people who thought of themselves as German.

3 Yugoslavia and Czechoslovakia were both 'new' countries containing a mixture of nationalities. What has happened to them in recent years?

Notice how much information a map can contain. Try drawing your own maps and colour code the individual countries to help with your revision.

Problems with the Treaty of Versailles

Germany also had to agree to other terms. At first the German government refused to accept the terms of the treaty, but was told that it had to. The US Congress thought the treaty was too severe, and refused to ratify it.

Source A

'You may strip Germany of her colonies, reduce her army to a mere police force and her navy to that of a fifth-rate power. All the same ... if she feels she has been unjustly treated ... she will find means of exacting retribution from her conqueror.'

Ex-Prime Minister Lloyd George: Speech, 1923

Source B

'The treaty was not so grand, I am quite willing to admit that, but how about the war? Was it so very grand? ... France came out of it alive, her territory recovered, her colonial empire increased, while Germany was broken and disarmed.'

Ex-French Prime Minister Clemençeau in an interview in 1928

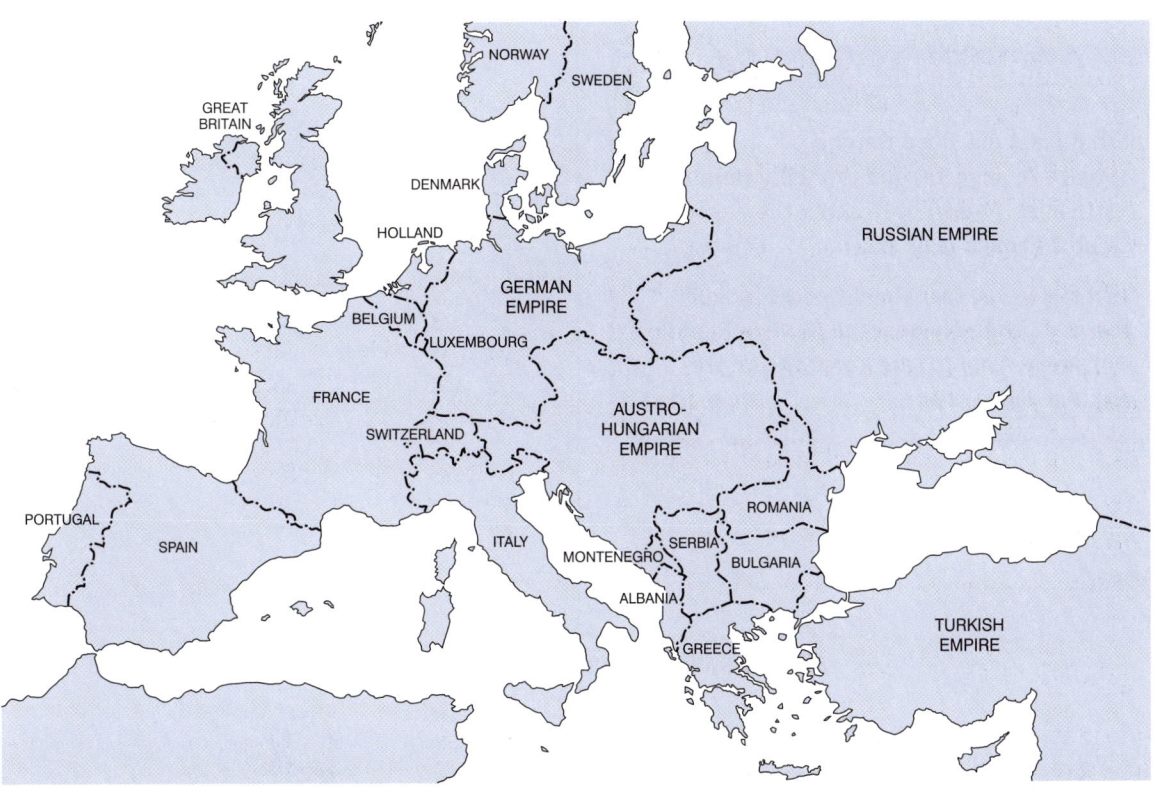

Europe before the 1919 treaties

Europe after the 1919 treaties

Specimen questions

1 What fears did Lloyd George (Source A, page 14) and the Daily Herald cartoonist (below) have about the peace treaty? Explain your answer. [6 marks]

2 Is it fair to say that Lloyd George looked forward, while Clemençeau (Source B, page 14) seemed not to care about the future? Explain your answer. [4 marks]

Source C

PEACE AND FUTURE CANNON FODDER

The Tiger: "Curious! I seem to hear a child weeping!"

A cartoon published in the Daily Herald. '1940 Class' refers to those who would be old enough to join the army to fight in 1940

Germany 1919–23

Popularity of the government

The fact that the new democratic German government (the Weimar Republic) had signed the Treaty of Versailles made it unpopular.

Specimen question

1 In what ways did the Treaty of Versailles limit Germany's military strength? [4 marks]

Hints

To earn four marks you need to mention four restrictions (e.g. no air force, no large battleships, no heavy artillery, no U-boats). Always notice the number of marks on offer. For four marks you will not be expected to write a long, full answer.

Specimen question

2 Why did the victors want to weaken Germany? [6 marks]

Hint

To earn six marks you need to give several reasons, explain them and link them together.

Model answer

The victors wanted to weaken Germany because they feared that there might be another war, and thought that weakening Germany was the best way of preventing one. They also wanted to punish Germany, whom they blamed for starting the war. Weakening Germany was a good way to punish her. So, for example, cutting Germany's armed forces and occupying the Rhineland seemed good ways to punish Germany and to protect France.

Specimen question

3 'Reparations were the most important reason why Germany hated the Treaty of Versailles.' Do you agree with this statement? Explain your answer. [10 marks]

Hints

If you deal only with the reason mentioned in a question like this, you will score less than half marks. To score full marks you need to explain that all or most of the terms of the treaty were unpopular in Germany, and that it is just not enough to pick out one 'most important' reason.

Model answer

Germans hated the Treaty of Versailles because it was a humiliation for their country and made some of them suffer. It was humiliating to lose their colonies and to have their army and navy reduced in size. It was humiliating to have to hand Alsace-Lorraine back to France, to lose Danzig and to have foreign troops occupying the Rhineland and the French running the Saar coalfields. It was also very humiliating to have to accept the blame for starting the war, and to have to pay reparations to the Allies when Germany needed money to rebuild its industries and provide jobs after the war. So all the terms of the treaty, coupled with the fact that it was imposed on them without asking what they thought, combined to make Germans hate it. It is wrong to single out one clause.

The economy

The German government also failed to control the country's economy.

Inflation timeline

1919	1 dollar = 14 marks.	
1921	Reparations fixed at £6,600 million.	
1922	German payments fell behind.	
1923	**January**	French and Belgian troops occupied the Ruhr to enforce payment.
		1 dollar = 18,000 marks.
	September	1 dollar = 98 million marks.
	November	1 dollar = 4200 billion marks.

Notes

When Germany's reparation payments fell behind and French and Belgian troops took over German factories and mines in the Ruhr, people thought that marks were certain to drop in value and sold them. This reduced their value.

To make up for this the German government printed more marks. This reduced their value still further, so even more were printed. And so the process went on, faster and faster.

Source A

'In the summer of that inflation year my grandmother . . . [sold] her house for I don't know how many thousands of millions of marks . . . Nothing was left except a pile of worthless pieces of paper when she died a few months later.'

Egon Larsen: *Weimar Eyewitness* (1976)

Source B

'All [ordinary people] knew was that a large bank account could not buy a straggly bunch of carrots . . . They knew that as individuals they were bankrupt. And they knew hunger when it gnawed at them, as it did daily. In their misery and their hopelessness they made the Republic the scapegoat for all that had happened.'

William L Shirer: *The Rise and Fall of the Third Reich* (1959)

Specimen question

Why, according to the sources, was the German government unpopular at the end of 1923? How far could this be blamed on the terms of the Treaty of Versailles? **[6 marks]**

Hint

As a rule in questions based on sources, you can use your general knowledge of the period in your answer. In this case, however, you must use only information contained in the sources when answering the first part of the question.

Check

That you understand the effect the Treaty of Versailles had on Germany.

The League of Nations
Establishment

The First World War was a catastrophe. It killed 10 million people and wounded 20 million. It was also very expensive. It cost Britain about £7000 million. To try to prevent further war, the Treaty of Versailles set up the League of Nations to settle disputes between countries by negotiation. The USA refused to join, and Germany, Russia and Turkey were excluded. The League could only use blockades to enforce its decisions. It had no armed forces at its disposal.

Organisation

Assembly
(all members)
made policy

agencies

agencies

international court

international labour office

Council
(4 permanent, 6 temporary members)

health organisation

mandates commission

Secretariat
carried out policies

Source A

THE GAP IN THE BRIDGE.

A cartoon published in *Punch* (10 December 1919)

Source B

Lord Robert Cecil, one of the founders of the League of Nations, wrote:

'*The governments had agreed to the covenant [of the League] without taking it seriously.
To them any genuine attempt to apply its provisions ... was "midsummer madness".*'

Viscount Cecil: Letter to Winston Churchill, 1944

Specimen question

1 **What does the cartoonist in Source A think about the League of Nations? Back up your answer by referring to details in the cartoon.** **[5 marks]**

Hints

What points is the cartoonist trying to make, and how does he use details in the cartoon to make them? For example, the League was greatly weakened by the absence of the USA – the missing keystone being the most important piece of the bridge. And though a US president, Woodrow Wilson, founded the League, as shown on the sign, the US government, lounging on the bank, were threatening the whole structure by refusing to join.

Specimen question

2   What did the Great Powers want the League of Nations to achieve?

[5 marks]

Hint

If you know a lot about the foundation of the League you could easily write too much on this. Remember, no matter how much you write, you won't get more than five marks. All that is needed for five marks is something like the following model answer.

Model answer

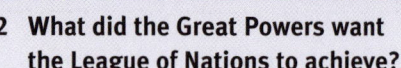

The Great Powers wanted the League to prevent wars by making sure that all disputes were settled by negotiation, and by making it easier for member states to band together to help other members if they were attacked. They also wanted the League to deal with other problems which arose from the peace treaties, such as controlling the administration of the mandated territories and dealing with refugees.

Specimen question

3   If Lord Cecil was right (Source B, page 19), could the League have ever succeeded? Explain your answer. [4 marks]

Check

That you understand the weaknesses of the League.

The League in the 1920s

Between 1919 and 1930 the League was involved in various disputes (*see* the table opposite).

Notes

*   Germany was annoyed in 1921 because the League handed over some German Silesians to be ruled by Poland.

*   The League's decision over Corfu was unpopular because many people believed that Italy won only because it was a permanent member of the Council and Greece was not.

*   Under the Dawes Plan (1924), the USA lent Germany money to pay reparations.

*   The League ordered Poland and Lithuania to negotiate over the future of Vilna, captured by Poland. Poland refused and kept Vilna.

*   The League tried to supervise the way in which the Allies administered 'mandated' territories. But they took no notice.

Specimen question

How successful was the League of Nations in settling disputes between 1920 and 1930? Explain your answer. [6 marks]

The League of Nations disputes, 1920s

Date	Place/Problem	Issue	Rivals	Result	Comment
1919	Alands	ownership	Sweden v Finland	Finland won	success
1920	Schleswig	ownership	Denmark v Germany	plebiscite split	success
1921	Silesia	ownership	Poland v Germany	plebiscite split	annoyed Germany
1922	S America	borders	Colombia v Venezuela	decided	success
1923	Corfu	compensation	Italy v Greece	Italy won	unpopular
1924	reparations	payment	Germany v Allies	Dawes Plan	success
1925	Balkans	Greek invasion	Greece v Bulgaria	Greeks withdrew	success
1925	S America	borders	Chile v Peru	decided	success
1926	Mosul	ownership	Iraq v Turkey	Iraq won	success
1927	Vilna	ownership	Poland v Lithuania	Poland won	League ignored
1920–30	mandates	supervision	League v Allies	no effect	League ignored

Hints

Approach this kind of question by making a statement and then giving an example. For instance, you could say that the League was very successful in settling minor disputes between small countries – give a couple of examples – but was helpless when one of the parties refused to do what it was told (e.g. Poland) or when it had to deal with stronger countries (e.g. Italy). In these cases it was shown to be weak and ineffective. So it was only partly successful.

Tip

Notice how much information a table can contain. Try compiling your own to help with your revision. You would not be expected to know details of all the disputes mentioned in the table above. Half a dozen or so will do.

The League of Nations 1930–39

After 1930 the League faced very difficult problems, which it could not solve:

- **Disarmament**
  Disarmament seemed a good way to prevent wars, so in 1929 the British Labour government persuaded the League to organise a disarmament conference which met from 1932 to 1934. It failed (see diagram below).

- **Manchuria**
  In 1931 Japan invaded Manchuria. China asked the League for help. The League set up a commission under Lord Lytton. This said that Japan should withdraw. Japan refused and left the League.

- **Abyssinia**
  In 1935 Mussolini, the Italian dictator, invaded Abyssinia, whose ruler, Haile Selassie, asked the League for help. In response, 52 nations agreed not to lend money or sell weapons to Italy. But they went on selling oil to Italy. Italy took over the whole country and resigned from the League.

Germany wanted to rearm. In 1933 Hitler came to power and withdrew from the League

Japan's invasion of Manchuria made people think disarmament was dangerous

Failure of conference

France wanted to keep strong enough forces to fight off Germany

A new **British** government elected in 1931 was against disarmament

THE ULTIMATUM.

JAPAN. "IF YOU GO ON SAYING I'M NAUGHTY, I SHALL LEAVE THE CLASS"

A cartoon published in *Punch* (7 December 1932)

Source B

'If the League . . . had extended sanctions to oil, I would have had to withdraw from Abyssinia within a week.' Mussolini, looking back on the invasion of Abyssinia

Source C

'This was the death-blow to the League as well as to Abyssinia. Fifty-two nations had combined to resist aggression; all they accomplished was that Haile Selassie lost all his country . . . One day [the League] was a powerful body imposing sanctions . . . the next day it was an empty sham.'

A J P Taylor: *The Origins of the Second World War* (1961)

Specimen question

1 Look at Source A. What impression does the artist give of the firmness shown by the League and Japan's reaction to the League? Explain your answer.   [5 marks]

Hint

Organise your answer along the lines of the model answer on page 20. Identify what points the cartoonist is trying to make, then show how he uses the details in the cartoon to make them.

Specimen question

2 What effects did the successful invasion of Manchuria have on world opinion?   [5 marks]

Hint

How effective would people think the League was? What effect would this have on leaders such as Mussolini thinking of aggression? What effect would it have on those fearing attack?

Specimen question

3 Look at Sources B and C.
   (a) How might the League have made sanctions against Italy more effective? Explain your answer.   [4 marks]
   (b) Why did A J P Taylor describe Abyssinia as 'the death-blow' to the League?   [5 marks]

Exam tip

When you are instructed to refer to a particular source to answer a question, you can also use your own knowledge and any of the other sources if they are relevant.

Check

That you can explain why the League of Nations had some success in the 1920s, but failed in the 1930s.

The Depression

In October 1929 the price of shares in US companies was higher than it had ever been. But the profits earned by companies were falling. It looked as if the price of shares might soon fall as well. So some shareholders decided to sell and the price of shares began to fall. Soon everybody was selling. Share prices fell faster and faster until many were almost worthless. Companies went bankrupt and many prosperous Americans suddenly found their investments worth nothing. This 'Wall Street Crash' had effects worldwide.

Specimen question

Why did the Wall Street Crash make it harder to prevent the outbreak of war between 1930 and 1939? Explain your answer fully.

[15 marks]

Hints

'Open-ended' questions like this are difficult to answer well. To achieve a high grade you need to show that you understand all aspects of the question, and be able to back up what you say with detailed evidence. The model answer is the kind of answer that would earn an A grade. Notice that it *selects* relevant information, which it uses to answer the question, and that it backs up general statements with particular examples.

Model answer

The Wall Street Crash caused a major slump in the USA. Many companies went bankrupt and by 1932, 12 million people were unemployed. This encouraged politicians such as Mussolini, Hitler and the Japanese generals, who all believed that democratic government did not work and were prepared to use force to get their way.

The slump spread all over the world. Countries stopped lending each other money because they feared they might not be repaid. This weakened democratic governments. During the 1920s the USA had lent money to Western Europe. Suddenly the USA wanted the money back. This hit Germany hard because she had borrowed more than 20,000 million marks

from the USA to pay her war reparations. Now she had no money to finance German trade and industry. By 1932, 44 per cent of German workers were unemployed. The Weimar government seemed helpless and many Germans voted instead for Hitler, who took power in 1933. In this way the Crash helped to bring to power the man who did most to bring about war in 1939.

The slump in trade caused by the Crash also hit France and Britain. By 1932 there were 3 million unemployed in Britain and well over a million in France. The British and French governments decided they could not afford to spend much on armaments. As a result they did not have the power or the confidence to oppose Mussolini when he invaded Abyssinia, or to stop Hitler when he occupied the Rhineland in 1936.

The Crash also affected the Pacific area, where Japan was trying to expand its influence. Before 1930 Japan did this by trading with other countries, but the slump after the Crash ruined these plans. So the Japanese government decided to use force instead, beginning with the invasion of Manchuria in 1931, believing that the USA was now too weak to stop them.

So, in various parts of the world, the Wall Street Crash helped to strengthen dictatorships and weaken democracies, making it more difficult to keep the peace.

Check

That you understand why the Depression made it more difficult to keep the peace.

German foreign policy 1924–39
The problems of the peace

Source

'First . . . the solution of the reparations question in a way that is tolerable for Germany, and the assurance of peace which is essential for us to recover our strength. Second, the protection of Germans abroad, those 10 to 12 million . . . who now live under foreign rule . . . The third great task is to recover Danzig, the Polish corridor and a correction of the frontier in Upper Silesia.'

Gustav Stresemann, the German Foreign Minister, writing of his aims in September 1925

The Locarno treaty

At the end of 1925 Stresemann signed a treaty at Locarno. He promised:

1   to allow France to keep Alsace-Lorraine
2   not to put troops into the Rhineland
3   not to use force to alter the frontiers of Poland and Czechoslovakia.

As a reward Germany was invited to join the League of Nations.

Specimen question

Many Germans agreed with Stresemann's aims. Do you think they would have been pleased by the treaty he signed at Locarno? Explain your answer.   [5 marks]

Hints

As a rule it is safest to give a balanced answer to this kind of question, looking for things which might have pleased the Germans – admission to the League of Nations, for example – as well as aspects which they might not have liked, such as the promises about the Rhineland and the other existing frontiers. Remember to refer back to Stresemann's aims as you go along. So you might decide that most Germans would have had mixed feelings about the treaty.

Just before he died in 1929, Stresemann agreed the Young Plan, which reduced the amount of reparations Germany had to pay by 70 per cent.

Hitler's policies

In 1933 Hitler came to power in Germany. By this time the League of Nations had lost much of its prestige. Hitler faced the same problems as Stresemann, but he took a very different line.

Source A

'I had no army worth mentioning . . . If the French had taken any action we would easily have been defeated.'

Hitler, speaking afterwards about the German occupation of the Rhineland

Source B

'The Germans, after all, are only going into their own back garden.'

Lord Lothian, a British politician, speaking of the Rhineland occupation

Source C

'Neither the British nor the French people were prepared to go to war to prevent German Austria from becoming a part of the German Reich. Indeed, there were many who believed that Austria, in the truncated form to which it had been reduced by the Treaty of Versailles, could not exist as an independent state.'

Lord Templewood: *Nine Troubled Years* (1954)

(Lord Templewood was a member of the British cabinet in 1938.)

Hitler's foreign policy timeline

1933		Hitler left the League of Nations, refused to pay any more reparations and began to rearm.
1936		Hitler broke the 1919 treaty by sending troops into the Rhineland. Nobody tried to stop him.
1938	**March**	Hitler broke the 1919 treaty by taking over Austria. Nobody tried to stop him.
	Sept	The Munich agreement, negotiated by Hitler and Chamberlain, allowed Germany to take over part of Czechoslovakia.
1939	**March**	Hitler took over the rest of Czechoslovakia. Nobody tried to stop him.
	August	Hitler signed a pact with the Soviet Union.
	Sept	Hitler invaded Poland. This started the Second World War.

Source D

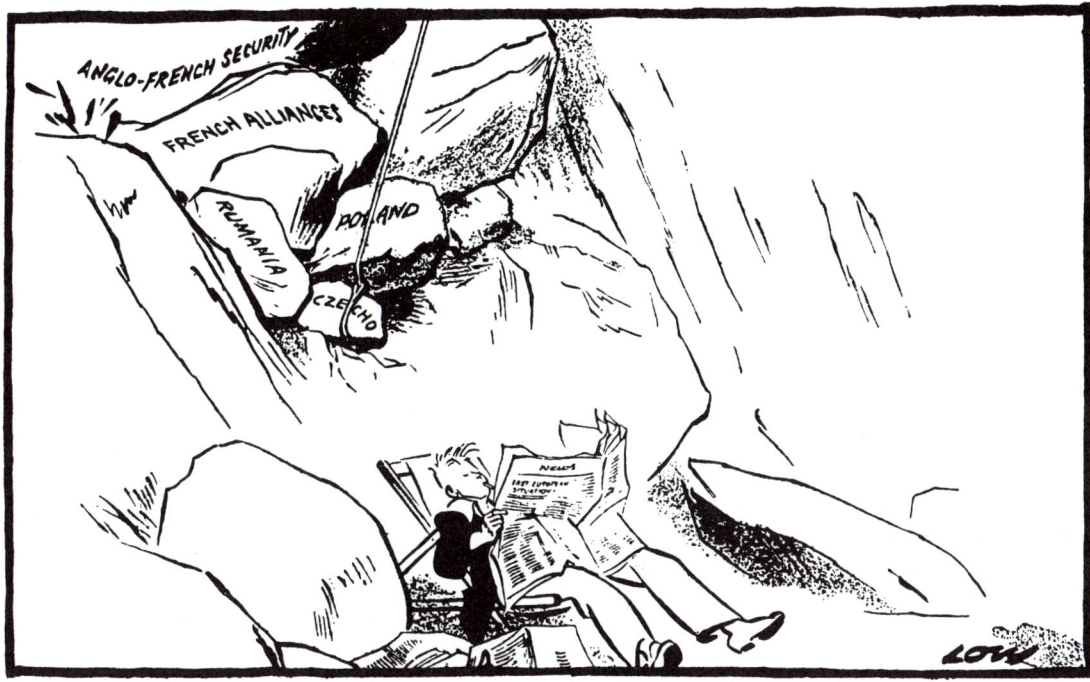

ANGLO-FRENCH SECURITY
FRENCH ALLIANCES
RUMANIA
POLAND
CZECHO
NEWS
LOW

WHAT'S CZECHOSLOVAKIA TO ME, ANYWAY ?

A cartoon drawn by David Low in 1938

Source E

'Czechoslovakia had a very weak moral and practical case in the matter of Sudetenland. [Fair-minded people] ... condemned that portion of the Peace Treaty which placed millions of Germans under Polish, Italian and Czech rule.'

Lord Winterton: *Orders of the Day* (1953)

(Lord Winterton was a member of the British cabinet in 1938.)

Source F

'Had Czechoslovakia defended herself we would have been held up by fortifications in the east, for we did not have the means to break through.'

Erich Von Manstein, a German general, speaking in 1946

Source G

'The year of respite from war which Munich afforded was perhaps the most valuable in our history for the defence of these islands. Without it, we should not have had the Hurricanes and Spitfires to win the Battle of Britain.'

Lord Winterton: *Orders of the Day* (1953)

Appeasement

Appeasement was the name given to British policy towards Hitler in the 1930s. It meant making concessions to Hitler in the hope that this would keep Europe at peace.

Specimen questions

1   Look at Source A. What, according to Hitler, would have happened if the French had opposed the German troops entering the Rhineland in 1936?   [2 marks]

2   What, do you think, did Lord Lothian mean when he said that the Germans were 'going into their own back garden' (Source B)?
    [4 marks]

3   Lord Templewood's account (Source C) of why Britain and France allowed Hitler to take over Austria in 1938 was written many years after the event. How reliable do you think it is for finding out about the events of 1938? Explain your answer.   [5 marks]

Hint

Notice the position Templewood held in 1938.

25

Model answer

As a member of the British cabinet which decided not to oppose Hitler, Templewood would want to show that the decision was justified. It is probably true that the British people opposed risking war to stop Hitler, but the idea that many people thought that Austria was too small to survive is difficult to prove. He does not say, even though it is true, that some ministers believed that Hitler was right to take over Austria. So the account is only partly reliable.

Specimen questions

4   Look at Sources D and E.
   (a) Did David Low, who drew the cartoon, agree with the attitude of the man in the deckchair? Explain your answer.
   [4 marks]
   (b) Both Lord Winterton and the character in the cartoon were against interfering to protect Czechoslovakia. How did their reasons differ?   [5 marks]

5   Read Sources F and G.
   (a) To what extent do they contradict each other?   [4 marks]
   (b) Which do you consider the more reliable? Explain your answer.
   [6 marks]

Check

That you understand what the British policy of appeasement was.

Model answer

(a) Sources F and G completely contradict each other. Winterton takes it for granted that in 1938 Britain, allied with Czechoslovakia, would not have been strong enough to go to war against Germany, while Von Manstein says that in 1938 Germany would not have been strong enough to defeat Czechoslovakia.

(b) Von Manstein is probably more reliable. Winterton, a member of Chamberlain's government in 1938, was trying to justify the decision not to help the Czechs, and in any case did not know as much as the German general Von Manstein about the strength of the German forces in 1938. Nor could he have been certain that, if war had broken out in 1938, a fight similar to the Battle of Britain would have taken place. Finally, Von Manstein had no reason not to tell the truth on this particular subject in 1946.

Specimen question

6   Is it fair to say that the main reason why France and Britain refused to act against Hitler before 1939 was that the 1919 treaty had treated Germany unfairly? Explain your answer fully.   [15 marks]

Hints

Remember to look for evidence *for* and *against* the view stated in the question. Sources B, C and E all contain evidence to support it, but Source G suggests that fear of the strength of Germany's forces played a part, while Source D shows that many people did not care. So perhaps the strictness of the treaty made people unwilling to enforce it, but indifference and fear of another war against Germany might have been just as important. Remember in History it is very difficult to be certain exactly *why* things happen.

The invasion of Poland

In the summer of 1939 Hitler was ready to attack Poland to win back the German land lost in the 1919 treaty. Britain and France had promised to support Poland if this happened. Hitler was ready to run this risk. But he feared that the Soviet Union, who had once owned much of Poland, might oppose him. So he began to negotiate with the Soviet government, and on 21 August the two countries signed a non-aggression pact, which contained a secret clause dividing Poland between them.

On 1 September German troops invaded Poland. Britain and France demanded that they withdraw. Hitler refused, so on 3 September 1939 France and Britain declared war on Germany.

Source A

'Everything I undertake is directed against Russia. If the West is too stupid and too blind to understand that, I will be forced to come to an understanding with the Russians, to smash the West and then . . . to turn against the Soviet Union.'

Hitler in conversation, 11 August 1939

Source B

'We knew that Hitler was trying to trick us with the treaty. I heard with my own ears Stalin say that because of this treaty the war would pass us by for a while longer. We would be able to stay neutral and save our strength.'

Nikita Khrushchev: *Khrushchev on Khrushchev* (1960)

(Khrushchev was a member of the Soviet government in 1939.)

Specimen question

1 Do you think Hitler was speaking the truth in Source A? Explain your answer. [4 marks]

Hints

Remember that Hitler was a great talker, who liked to impress or even shock his listeners and was therefore likely to exaggerate. But also remember his plans for *Lebensraum* and what in fact happened in the war.

Specimen question

2 What did Hitler and Stalin gain from the Nazi–Soviet pact? [4 marks]

Background to the Nazi–Soviet pact

The alliance between Hitler and the USSR might not have happened.

Source A

'My general impression is that the Soviet government are at present determined to conclude an agreement with Britain and France if they fulfil all Soviet wishes.'

Schulenburg, German ambassador to Moscow: Dispatch to Berlin, 4 August 1939

Source B

'If we are going in [to promise to help Poland] without the help of Russia we are walking into a trap. It is the only country whose arms can get there.'

Lloyd George: House of Commons speech, April 1939

Source C

'Chamberlain [Britain's Prime Minister] never wanted association with the Soviet Union except on impossible terms.'

A J P Taylor: *The Origins of the Second World War* (1961)

Specimen question

What evidence is there in the sources that Britain, France and the USSR might have made a treaty if Chamberlain had not been Prime Minister? Explain your answer. [6 marks]

Check

That you understand how Hitler's policies led to war in 1939.

Preview

What you need to know:

- **Why a revolution broke out in 1905, how the Tsar dealt with it, and what followed**

- **Why a revolution took place in March 1917, and what followed it**

- **How the Bolsheviks seized power in October 1917**

- **The system of government set up by Lenin, the civil war which followed the revolution, and Lenin's policies**

- **How Stalin came to power and how he used it**

A note on dates

Until 1918 the Russian calendar was thirteen days behind the rest of Europe. In this book the dates are modernised.

The 1905 Revolution

Causes

In 1904 war broke out between Japan and Russia. In December 1904 the Japanese captured the Russian naval base of Port Arthur. In January 1905 a revolution broke out in Russia.

Location of Port Arthur

Source A

'What little my parents earned was spent on bread. Thanks to the neighbours we were sometimes given porridge or cabbage soup. This was the usual tradition amongst the peasants of Russia, who all knew what it was like to live in great need.'

Marshal Georgi Zhukov: *Memories and Reflections* (1965)

Source B

'Coal, iron, oil and textile industries all existed ... Most of these workers lived in wretched poverty, inhabiting poor homes and working long hours.'

S H Wood: *World Affairs 1900 to the Present Day* (1970)

Specimen question

Give three possible causes of the 1905 Revolution in Russia. Explain your answer.

[5 marks]

Hint

The sources and the introduction give you all the information you need. Why was it likely that many people would want to get rid of the government in Russia in 1905?

The events of the Revolution

1905 Revolution timeline

22 January	(Bloody Sunday) Troops in St Petersburg fired on a peaceful demonstration.
28 June	Crew of battleship *Potemkin* mutinied.
October	General strike all over western Russia. Tsar promised an elected '*Duma*' (Parliament) with a Prime Minister. This split the Revolutionaries. Then the Tsar restored order.

Source A

'**Now at last my people and I are at peace**',
says the Tsar.
This cartoon appeared in a Russian magazine in 1906

Source B

'*By the time the Tsar was compelled to summon the first Duma in April 1906, it is estimated that his government had killed some 15,000 people and arrested 70,000.*'

David Thomson: *Europe Since Napoleon* (1966)

Specimen questions

1 **How did the Tsar's government restore order?** [3 marks]

2 **Did the cartoonist of Source A approve or disapprove of the Tsar's actions? Explain your answer.** [5 marks]

Hint

You need to explain how the cartoonist made his feelings clear in his drawing.

Specimen question

3 **To what extent does the author of Source B confirm the impression given by Source A?** [3 marks]

The Dumas

In 1905 the Tsar gave way to demands for a parliament or Duma elected by the people: workers, landowners, peasants and townspeople. But the Duma had limited power. It:

- could not pass laws
- could not appoint ministers
- could not control finance
- could be dissolved by the Tsar whenever he chose.

Duma timeline

First Duma **May–July 1906**	Dissolved – too critical of Tsar.
Second Duma **March–June 1907**	Dissolved – too critical of Tsar.
(Electoral system then altered, giving more power to the upper classes.)	
Third Duma **1907–12**	Uncritical – ran full term.
Fourth Duma **1912–17**	Criticised war policy. Tsar dissolved it.

Tip

Notice how much information can be crammed into a table. Compile your own to help your revision.

Source A

'*In my mind his Majesty the Emperor is the anointed of God ... When the will of such a man is made clear ... loyal subjects must submit, no matter what the consequences.*'

I Goremykin, Prime Minister of Russia: Speech, 1906

Source B

'*Let it be known that I, devoting all my strength to the pursuit of the good of my people, will maintain the principle of autocracy.*'

Tsar Nicholas II: Speech, 1894

Source C

'*The Duma ... retained the right to examine the greater part of the budget. Every Minister, therefore, ... was bound to seek its goodwill.*'

Sir Bernard Pares: *A History of Russia* (1947)

Specimen question

Why was Tsar Nicholas II unable to work with the Dumas between 1906 and 1914? Explain your answer. **[6 marks]**

Hints

Note that the Tsar believed in 'autocracy' – that is, one person having complete control. Notice, too, the attitude of his Prime Minister. How do these match up with the idea that the Duma had the 'right', for instance, to examine the budget?

Check

That you can explain why revolution occurred in 1905, how the Tsar dealt with it, and how it affected the government of Russia.

The March 1917 Revolution

In August 1914 the First World War began, and the Russian army was mobilised and went to war. By the middle of September they had been defeated in two battles, at Tannenberg and the Masurian Lakes, and had lost more than 200,000 men. In 1915 the Tsar took personal control of the army.

Source A

'[In 1914] troops were embarking for the front. A packed train was on the point of leaving. Inside the young faces of the soldiers were cheerful. They were singing rousing marching songs . . . A wave of fervent patriotism swept over Russia.'

Eugenie Fraser: *The House by the Dvina* (1984)

(Eugenie Fraser lived in Russia until 1920. In 1984 she wrote her memoirs, *The House by the Dvina*.)

Source B

In 1916 a wounded soldier visited Eugenie Fraser's home. He said:

'Some of us were defending mother Russia with our bare hands – lucky to lift a rifle from a dead comrade . . . I've had enough, the stink of death, the rotting bodies, flies, maggots – and all for what? For nothing . . . Russia is finished.'

Source C

Facts and figures

	1914	1915	1916	1917
Prices (%)	100	125	130	400
Bread ration		2.5 lb	2 lb	1.5 lb
Size of army	5.5 m	10 m	15 m	36 m

Source D

A contemporary cartoon, showing Rasputin

Source E

'Everybody was fed up with the Tsar because they thought he was weak . . . He was much criticised. There were lots of scandals at court.'

Margot Tracey, daughter of a wealthy businessman living in Russia at the time: Television interview, 1990

Source F

'Don't yield. Be the boss. Obey your firm little wife and Our Friend [Rasputin]. Believe in us.'

Letter from Tsarina to Nicholas II, 1916

March 1917 Revolution timeline

8 March	Strikes in Petrograd, protesting against food shortages. Mutinies in the army.
12 March	Workers and soldiers in Petrograd elected a '*Soviet*' (committee) to represent them. The Tsar's ministers fled.
15 March	Nicholas II, trapped in his train on his way to Petrograd, met delegates from the Duma and a number of generals. All advised him to abdicate. He did, and power passed to the leaders of the Duma and the Soviet.

Specimen question

1 Was Nicholas II to blame for the March 1917 Revolution? Explain your answer fully, using both the sources and your own knowledge. [15 marks]

Hints

Always be suspicious of one simple explanation for events. But beware of just listing the causes of the Revolution. To get really good marks you need to use the sources to back up your opinion of how far Nicholas was to blame.

Model answer

In theory, Nicholas was to blame because he had been in sole charge of Russia since 1894. But, in fact, some of the problems were not entirely his fault.

The army's lack of equipment which angered soldiers (Source B) after they had been so patriotic in 1914 (Source A) was due to Russia's inefficient industry and administration. This would have been difficult for Nicholas to correct, and he could not be blamed for short rations and high prices in Petrograd, which were partly caused by the number of peasants taken off the land to serve in the army (Source C). After all, Nicholas was away with the army.

But he *was* to blame for allowing the unpopular (Source D) and scandalous (Source E) Rasputin too much influence. Source E says that people thought Nicholas was weak. This view is backed up by Source F, which shows that the Tsarina thought he needed firm encouragement.

The feeling that a weak man was in charge at such a time must have encouraged people to get rid of him. So, though Nicholas could not be directly blamed for the immediate causes of the Revolution, his character and some of his actions made it much more likely.

Tip

Now, using the same sources and your own knowledge, try to answer question 2.

Specimen question

2 Do you agree that the 1917 March Revolution was caused by the grievances of the workers? Explain your answer fully. [15 marks]

The provisional government

A new provisional government, headed by a nobleman, Prince Lvov, replaced the Tsar.

Source A

'[The Government's] orders are executed only insofar as this is permitted by the Soviet of Workers' and Soldiers' Deputies which holds in its hands the most important elements of actual power, such as troops, railways, postal and telegraph services.'

A L Guchov, Defence Minister, in a letter, April 1917

Source B

'Lynch law, the destruction of houses and shops ... unauthorised arrests, seizures and beatings-up were recorded every day by tens and hundreds ... The soldiers, without leave, went off home in great floods.'

N Sukhanov, a Menshevik leader: *Memoirs* (1955)

Source C

'When [the government] promise you a lot they are deceiving you and the whole Russian people. The people needs peace; the people needs bread; the people needs land. And they give war, hunger, no bread – leave the landlords still in the land.'

V Lenin: Speech, April 1917

Specimen questions

1 Which do you think had more power after the March Revolution – the Soviet or the provisional government? Explain your answer. **[4 marks]**

2 What evidence is there that the provisional government could not:
   (a) control the army
   (b) enforce law and order? **[3 marks]**

3 Do you think Lenin's criticism of the provisional government was fair? Explain your answer. **[4 marks]**

Hint

Remember, when answering question 3, that the government was provisional and temporary.

Check

That you understand why a revolution happened in March 1917 and why the provisional government which followed it was so weak.

The Bolshevik Revolution

In 1903 there was a meeting of the Russian Social Democratic Party in London. The Party split. The majority (in Russian, the Bolshevik) wanted violent revolution. The minority (in Russian, the Menshevik) wanted gradual change.

By the middle of 1917 the Bolsheviks, led by Lenin and Trotsky (a former Menshevik), had seized control of the Russian government from the democratic Prime Minister, Kerensky. How were they able to do this?

Source A

'Either we must abandon our slogan "All power to the Soviets", or else we must make an insurrection. There is no middle course.'

V Lenin: Speech, 31 October 1917

Source B

All power to the Soviets

Immediate truce on all fronts

Landlord estates ... to the peasants

Workers' control over industrial production

An ... honestly elected Constituent Assembly

Demands published in *Rabochi i Soldat*, a Bolshevik newspaper, 17 October 1917

Source C

'The inflated puppets of the Winter Palace understood nothing. Thinking themselves strong, they felt no alarm ... They told each other that steps had been and would be taken ... and [did] nothing else.'

N K Sukhanov, a socialist journalist, writing in his memoirs (1955) about the provisional government

Specimen questions

Read the timeline (below) and the sources on page 32. What evidence is there in them that:

(a) Trotsky was a good organiser and a clever plotter

(b) the Bolsheviks had policies which would appeal to many peasants, soldiers and industrial workers

(c) Lenin was a clear and decisive leader

(d) the provisional government was weak and indecisive? **[15 marks]**

October 1917 (Bolshevik) Revolution timeline

September	General Kornilov tried to overthrow Kerensky. The Bolsheviks helped to defeat him and took control of the Petrograd Soviet.
12 October	Petrograd Soviet appointed a military committee under Trotsky to 'defend the revolution'.
25 October	Trotsky obtained 5000 rifles to equip a 'Red Army of workers'.
3 November	Trotsky appointed a Soviet commissar to liaise with every regiment in Petrograd. Told the troops to obey the commissar, not their officers.
5 November	Trotsky distributed arms and ordered troops to take over strong points in the city. Kerensky ordered his arrest and that of Lenin.
7 November	Kerensky left Petrograd. All-Russian Congress of Soviets, called by the Petrograd Soviet, took charge.
8 November	Bolsheviks captured the Winter Palace.
13 November	Bolshevik army defeated Kerensky's forces. Kerensky fled abroad.

Lenin's government

The Soviet system

The Bolsheviks set up a new system of government dominated by the Communist Party.

State	Party
Local Soviets	Local Party members
elect	elect
Regional Soviets	The Party Congress
elect	elects
All Russian Congress of Soviets	The Central Committee
elects	elects
COUNCIL OF MINISTERS (which can make new laws)	**THE POLITBURO** (which makes all important decisions)

Only people approved by the Communist Party could stand for office. They called the new state the Union of Soviet Socialist Republics (USSR).

Specimen question

Supporters of the Soviet Union claimed that the Soviet system was democratic. Opponents said it was not. How could both have justified their views? **[6 marks]**

The Cheka

The Bolsheviks set up a secret police – the Cheka – to enforce their policies.

Source A

'The Cheka is the defence of the revolution . . . as the Red Army cannot stop to ask whether it may harm particular individuals . . . so the Cheka must . . . conquer the enemy even if its sword falls occasionally on the heads of the innocent.'

The Head of the Cheka at a press conference in 1918

'People we knew vanished from the face of the earth. Those living near the outskirts of the town saw, in the early hours of the morning, prisoners taken by the back streets to the woods, and heard the sounds of shots as they were summarily executed.'

Eugenie Fraser: *The House by the Dvina* (memoirs) (1984)

Specimen question

1 Eugenie Fraser's family were industrialists in Russia. Does this make her account more or less likely to be true? Explain your answer. **[5 marks]**

Hints

Was she an eyewitness of the events she describes? Was she likely to approve of the revolution? Might she have checked carefully on stories of mysterious shootings at the time, or exaggerated them as the years passed?

Specimen question

2 Does the statement by the Head of the Cheka (Source A, page 33) make you more or less likely to believe Eugenie Fraser's account? Explain your answer. **[4 marks]**

Check

That you understand the Soviet system of government.

The Treaty of Brest Litovsk

In December 1917 Trotsky began to negotiate with the German government for a peace treaty. In March 1918 they signed the Treaty of Brest Litovsk.

Source

Land lost by the USSR in the Treaty of Brest Litovsk

Specimen question

Does the source confirm Lenin's view that Brest Litovsk was a 'robber peace'? Explain your answer. **[5 marks]**

Hints

Notice the huge area lost by Russia. But remember the Bolsheviks' slogans about the need for peace. Remember the political systems in Germany and Russia. Were the Germans justified in taking all they could?

Check

That you can explain the terms of the Treaty of Brest Litovsk.

The Civil War 1918–22

After the Revolution the Bolshevik government had to fight a civil war which they finally won in 1922. Their opponents were known as the 'Whites'.

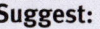

Tip

Maps combined with notes can hold a lot of information. Draw your own to help with your revision.

Specimen question

Suggest:

(a) two advantages which helped the Reds to win

(b) two disadvantages which led the Whites to lose

(c) three countries which helped the Whites. Suggest reasons why they may have done so. **[10 marks]**

War Communism

The Soviet government had handed over land to the peasants, and factories to the workers. They allowed peasants to keep enough food for their families, and ordered them to hand over the rest to the State.

Source A

'Every grain collection squad must have at least 75 men with two or three machine guns.'

Instruction to grain collection squads, August 1918

Source B

'The workers of the towns and some of the villages choke in the throes of hunger. The railroads barely crawl. The houses are crumbling. The towns are full of refuse. Epidemics spread and death strikes to the right and to the left. Industry is ruined.'

Pravda, Communist Party newspaper, 26 February 1920

Source C

'Workers and peasants are so enfeebled that they are almost incapable of work.'

V Lenin: Speech to 1921 Communist Party Congress

Specimen question

1 Suggest two reasons why the grain collection squads had to be armed.

[3 marks]

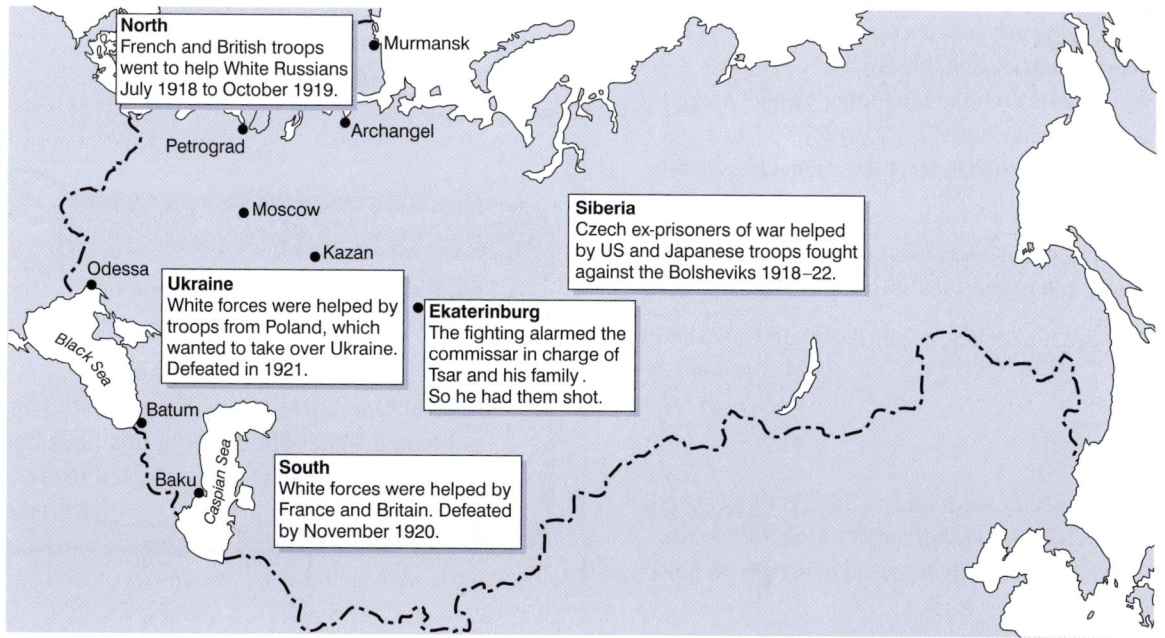

The main events of the Civil War

Hint

Think of the attitude of the peasants and the general shortage of food.

Specimen question

2 In 1921 sailors at the Baltic naval base of Kronstadt rebelled against the Soviet government. Use the sources and your own knowledge to explain why they did so. [10 marks]

Hints

The Soviet government had promised to improve life for the Russian people. Had it done so? If not, in what ways was life worse? How might this have made the sailors at Kronstadt decide to try to overthrow the government?

The New Economic Policy

Lenin decided that War Communism was not working. So he introduced a new economic policy. Its main features were:

- grain requisitioning was halted
- peasants had to give a fixed amount of grain to the government each year (as tax) – surplus could be sold
- traders could sell and buy goods
- small factories returned to former owners and allowed to make a profit
- large industries (coal, steel, etc.) remained under state control

Production of goods and foodstuffs increased. But in 1923 it was still below 1914 levels. In 1924 Lenin died.

In 1925 Maynard Keynes, a British economist, visited the USSR.

> Source

'So, now the deeds are done and there is no going back … Even allowing for everything, if I were a Russian … I [would rather] contribute my quota of activity to Soviet Russia than to Tsarist Russia.'

J M Keynes: *A Short View of Russia* (1925)

Specimen questions

1 What actions taken by Lenin and the Bolsheviks may Keynes have been thinking of when he says 'even allowing for everything'? [4 marks]

2 What examples of life in Russia before and after the Revolution might Keynes have given in 1925 to support his judgement? [6 marks]

Check

That you can explain how War Communism and the New Economic Policy differed.

Stalin and the USSR

Stalin comes to power

There were at least four men who might have taken power in the USSR on Lenin's death in 1924. They were Trotsky, Kamenev, Zinoviev and Stalin, who was General Secretary of the Soviet Communist Party. Lenin left a will, which mentioned Stalin.

> Source A

'Stalin, having become General Secretary, has concentrated enormous power in his hands … I propose that the comrades find a way to remove Stalin from the position and appoint another man, loyal, more courteous, more considerate, etc.'

V Lenin: *Will*

Specimen questions

1 What weaknesses did Lenin see in Stalin? [2 marks]

2 Lenin's will was read out to the Party Central Committee. Many expected it to be published. What effect would this have had on Stalin's chance of being elected leader? [2 marks]

Stalin's tactics

Many people thought that Trotsky, still in charge of the Red Army, should be the new leader, but some long-serving Bolsheviks did not trust him because he joined the Bolsheviks only in 1917. So when Stalin offered to help Kamenev and Zinoviev to defeat Trotsky they willingly agreed. In return they agreed to help Stalin to suppress Lenin's will. So it was never published.

Meanwhile Stalin, Kamenev and Zinoviev persuaded the Central Committee to put Trotsky in charge of the electrification of the USSR. This meant he had to resign as Commander in Chief of the Red Army, which was the basis of his power. All the while, Stalin was using his position as General Secretary to increase his support on the Central Committee.

When he was ready, Stalin turned on Kamenev and Zinoviev. His supporters voted them and Trotsky off the Politburo and the Central Committee. Then in 1927 they were voted out of the Party. By 1928 Stalin was in complete control.

Specimen question

Read the account of how Stalin got to power. Would his methods have inspired affection, respect, or fear? Explain your answer. [5 marks]

Check

That you understand how Stalin came to power.

Stalin's industrial policies

Stalin wanted to turn the USSR into a great industrial power and he instituted a Five Year Plan to achieve this. See the spider diagram to remind yourself of the main features.

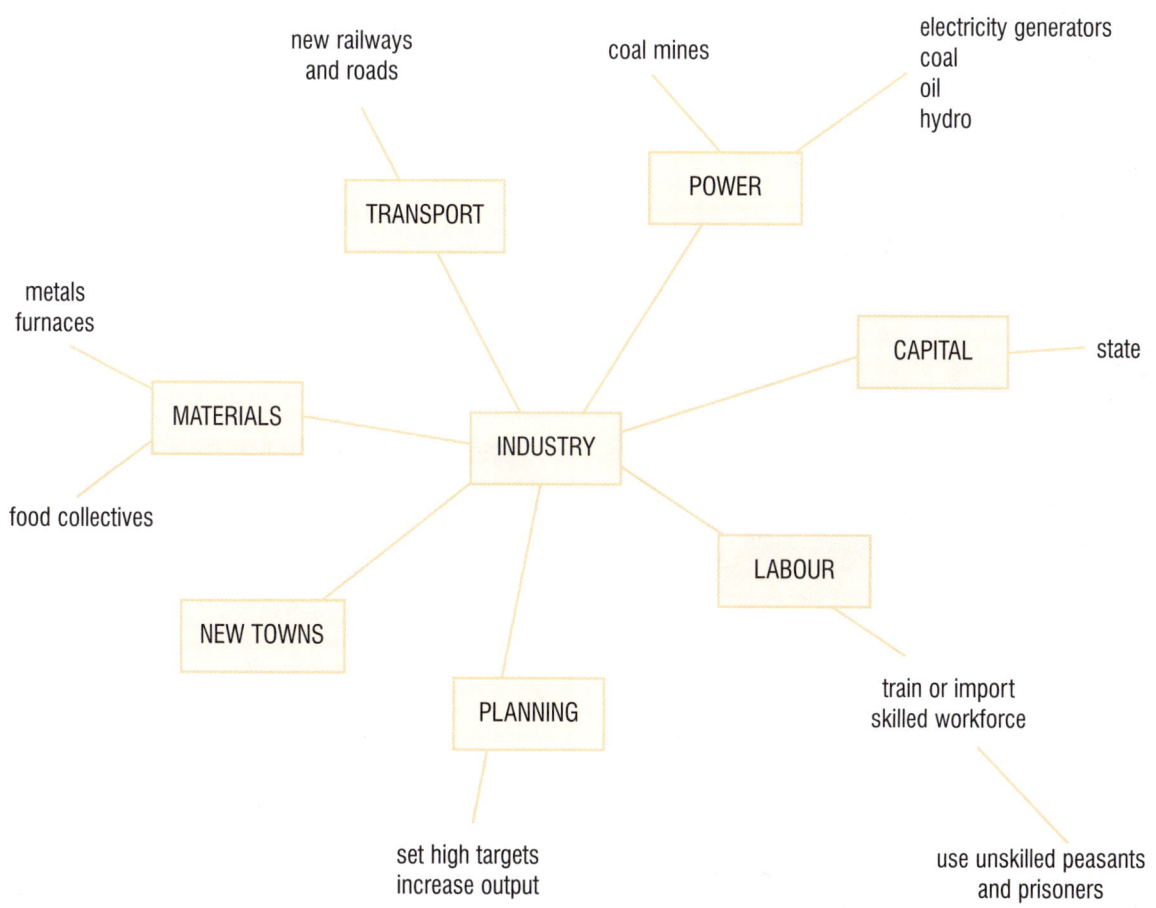

'We are 50 or 100 years behind the advanced countries. We must make good the lag in ten years. Either we do it or they will crush us.'

Stalin: Speech, 1931

Source B

'How was it possible at one of the most difficult times to raise these great construction sites? It was only possible through the unity of the people and the love of the people for their idol, because for us Stalin was an idol.'

Tatiana Fedorova, 1930s construction worker: Documentary film, 1995

Source C

A Soviet propaganda poster, published in 1931

Source D

'In early April it was still bitter cold, everything was frozen solid. By May the city was swimming in mud. Bubonic Plague had broken out not far from Magnitogorsk. The resistance of the population was very low because of under-nourishment and consistent overwork. Sanitary conditions were appalling … We were consumed by bed bugs and other vermin.'

John Scott: *Behind the Urals* (1942)

(John Scott was an American welder, working in the new town of Magnitogorsk.)

Specimen questions

1 Why did Stalin think it vital for the USSR to catch up quickly (Source A)?
   [2 marks]

2 Did he prove to be right? Explain your answer.
   [4 marks]

3 Source C is a 1931 poster designed to attract women to work in industrial centres. To what extent is its message contradicted by the information in Source D? Which is more reliable? Explain your answer.
   [6 marks]

4 Was Tatiana Fedorova (Source B) right to think that the construction sites were built because of the 'unity of the people' inspired by their 'idol' Stalin? Explain your answer.
   [10 marks]

Hint

What about fear, orders from the top, foreign help (e.g. John Scott), forced labour, etc?

The results of industrialisation

Production (millions of tons)		
	1929	**1940**
Coal	40	164
Iron and steel	9	36
Oil	13	34
(Soviet statistics)		

Source B

'1938 [Magnitogorsk] ... did boast 50 schools, 3 colleges, 2 large theatres, half a dozen small ones, 17 libraries, 22 clubs, 18 clinics ... A large park had been constructed in 1935.'

John Scott: *Behind the Urals* (1942)

Specimen question

1 **Does Source A prove that Stalin's industrial policy was a success? Explain your answer.** [6 marks]

Hints

Remember that it is difficult to prove most things. Consider what happened to production. Is this what Stalin wanted? Might other methods have worked better? Are the figures reliable? Come to a conclusion.

Specimen question

2 **How does Source B support the view that Stalin had the interests of Soviet workers at heart?** [3 marks]

Check

That you understand the changes Stalin wanted to make in the USSR's industry and how far he achieved them.

The collectivisation of agriculture

Industrial towns needed a reliable supply of food. Lenin's New Economic Policy did not provide it because the peasants could decide how much they would sell to the State. In addition, peasants with their small farms could not afford to improve their land or buy the latest machinery. So they produced very little to send to the towns.

Source A

'The way out is to unite the small and dwarf peasant farms gradually but surely, not by pressure but by example and persuasion into large farms based on the common co-operative cultivation of the land. There is no other way out.'

Stalin: Speech to Communist Party Congress, 1927

Source B

'We have passed to the policy of eliminating the kulaks as a class ... We must strike at the kulaks, strike so hard as to prevent them rising to their feet again. We must annihilate them as a social class.'

Stalin: Speech to Communist Party Congress, 1929

Source C

'The majority of kulaks were deported to uninhabited areas in the East. There they were left ... homeless, without food, tools or seed. The great majority died from starvation, disease and exposure.'

E M Roberts: *Stalin: Man of Steel* (1968)

Specimen questions

1 **Read Source A. How did Stalin intend to overcome the problem of low food production?** [3 marks]

2 **Did Stalin expect serious opposition to his policy? Explain your answer.** [8 marks]

Model answer

Stalin must have known that peasants who had been given their land as a result of the Bolshevik Revolution would not want to hand it over to a collective farm. But in 1927 he seemed to think that the holders of 'small and dwarf' plots could be persuaded to give up their land by gradual, peaceful methods. By 1929 he was convinced that the kulaks, rich peasants who had more to lose, would never be persuaded. He thought the only way to get their land was to annihilate them as a social class. So he expected little opposition from poor peasants, but determined opposition from the kulaks.

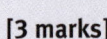

Specimen question

3 What does the fate of the kulaks tell us about Stalin's character? **[3 marks]**

Collectivisation in action

Stalin altered the system of collecting food from the peasants. Officials decided how much each collective had to contribute, and allowed the peasants to keep only what was left.

Source A

'*Both those who joined the collective and the individual farmers killed their stock. Bulls, sheep, pigs, even cows were slaughtered, as well as cattle for breeding. "Kill, it's not ours any more . . . Kill, they will take it for meat anyway." '*

M Sholokov: *Virgin Soil Upturned* (a novel) (1940)

Source B

An official photograph of peasants queuing to join a collective

Source C

'*We've eaten everything we could lay our hands on – cats, dogs, field mice, birds . . . You will see that the trees have been stripped of their bark, for that too has been eaten. And the horse manure has been eaten, we fight over it. Sometimes there are whole grains in it.'*

A peasant in the village of Petrovo, reporting to Viktor Kravchenko, a party worker sent to collect the grain quota

Source D

Agricultural statistics

	Grain (millions of tons)		Livestock (millions)	
	Harvest	To towns	Pigs	Cattle
1928	73	11	26	60
1930	83	22		
1932	70	19		
1934	68	26	12	30

Notes

In Source D, the figures under 'Harvest' in the grain table give the total grain harvest in millions of tons. The figures under 'To towns' give the amount sent to feed those living in the towns.

In the livestock table the figures give the total number of pigs and cattle in the USSR in the year in question.

Figures are only approximate.

Specimen questions

1 What impressions do (a) Source A, and (b) Source B give of the peasants' feelings about collectivisation? Explain your answers. **[5 marks]**

2 Do Sources C and D tend to support Source A or Source B? Explain your answer. **[4 marks]**

3 What do we have to take into account about (a) Source A, (b) Source B and (c) Source C when trying to decided how reliable each of them is? **[6 marks]**

Hints

Who wrote/produced/said them?
What impressions might they have been trying to make?

Specimen question

4 Did collectivisation fulfil Stalin's aims? Explain your answer. **[10 marks]**

Hints

Look at the figures in Source D. What happened to food production? Would this have pleased Stalin? What happened to the amount of food going to the towns? Would this have pleased Stalin? Who suffered as a result of collectivisation? Would Stalin have cared? Evidence for this?

Check

That you understand why Stalin wanted collectivisation, how it was imposed, and what the effects were.

Stalin in power

Stalin controlled every aspect of Soviet life (see diagram below). He used his control over the media and the system of justice to maintain his hold on power.

Source

'We live so well. Our hearts are so joyful. In no other country are there such happy young people as us . . . and on behalf of all young people I want to thank our party and our dear comrade Stalin for this joy we have.'

Tatiana Fedorova in a 1932 Soviet propaganda film

Specimen questions

1 What was the aim of the piece of soundtrack spoken by Tatiana Fedorova in 1932? [2 marks]

2 Which young people in the USSR would probably not have had 'joyful hearts' in 1932? Explain your answer. [4 marks]

3 Study the spider diagram (below) and the source. Compare them with Sources A and B on page 29. In what ways was the position of Stalin (a) similar to and (b) different from that of Tsar Nicholas? [5 marks]

Hints

Uncritical admiration? Determination to retain power? Role of religion.

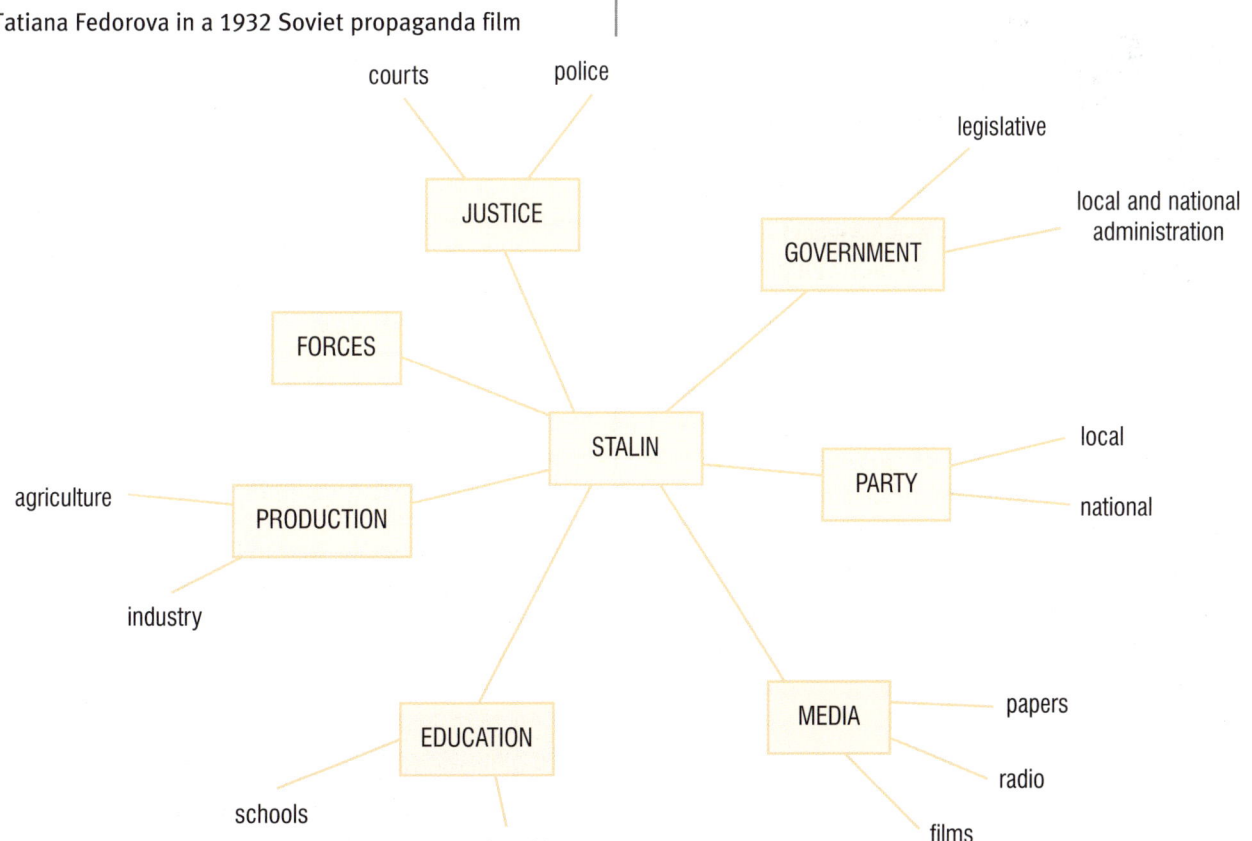

Silencing opposition

After 1934 Stalin used mass arrests, show trials, executions and deportations to labour camps to get rid of his opponents. Between 1934 and 1941, 30 million were arrested, of whom about 16 million died or were executed.

Source A

'Thousands and thousands of corpses were buried in more than 500 mass graves. The massacres were carried out over four years from 1937 ... Residents ... could not sleep at night for the sound of machine guns ... The victims covered all professions, from engineers and teachers to soldiers and communist party workers. They were all branded under the common term "enemy of the people" and shot by the NKVD.'

Alex Adamovitch, Belorussian journalist, quoted in the *Guardian*, 26 September 1988

Source B

'Before dawn we were marched to a bleak open field. Until 1 pm we hacked at the frozen soil with spades. We ate between 1 pm and 1.30 at the camp, trying to warm ourselves over the stove. From 1.30 pm until 8 pm we worked again.'

Eugenia Ginzberg, a political prisoner for eighteen years: *Into the Whirlwind* (1981)

Source C

'When he said, "You can't imagine it, Stalin is shooting all the present members of the Politburo!", and he counted them off one by one, I couldn't bear it. We were having lunch. I picked up a knife and threw it at him.'

Ella Shistyer, speaking of her first husband in a 1995 documentary.

(He was later killed by the secret police. Ella was later imprisoned in Siberia.)

Source D

'What would you have said in my place if you had heard a man confess his crimes with your own ears?'

Boris Yeminov, a political cartoonist who attended the 1930s treason trials, in a 1995 documentary

Specimen questions

1 Are Sources A and B good evidence that Stalin was using terror tactics against his opponents between 1934 and 1941? **[6 marks]**

2 Why did Ella Shistyer find it so hard to accept her husband's accusations against Stalin? Refer to Source D and use your own knowledge. **[4 marks]**

Hint

Think about the power of propaganda.

Check

That you understand the methods which Stalin used to stay in power.

Conclusion

In 1941 Hitler invaded the USSR. It held out against his forces and in the end defeated them. Here are two views of Stalin's work.

Source A

'He was the greatest enemy of Socialism. He had damaged Socialism by destroying people in all parts of life, in agriculture, the arts, the military, the party. He destroyed people everywhere. Wasn't that evil?'

Mikhail Mindlin, a political prisoner 1937–54, in a 1995 documentary

Source B

'As I think back, I ask myself, again and again: was there an alternative to the indiscriminate, brutal, basically unplanned rush forward of the first Five Year Plan? I wish I could say there was, but I cannot. I cannot find an answer.'

Oskar Lange, a socialist economist, quoted by Eric Hobsbawm in *Age of Extremes* (1994)

Specimen question

Should the Soviet Union have been grateful to Stalin? Explain your answer fully.
[15 marks]

Hints

This question needs you to strike a balance. What did Stalin do that was good for the Soviet Union, and what did he do that damaged it, and which outweighed the other? You should consider the way he built up Soviet industry. Could the USSR have been strong enough to resist Germany in 1941 without his work? On the other hand, what was his effect on Soviet agriculture and on political life in the USSR? Come to a conclusion. Use the sources and the information in this section to help you.

Preview

What you need to know:

- **American society between 1918 and 1929, when sections of it were very prosperous**

- **Why the US government banned alcoholic drinks and what the results were**

- **Why the price of American stocks and shares rose, and then suddenly fell in October 1929, and what the results were**

- **Why the Great Depression happened, and how it affected American society**

- **How President Roosevelt tackled the Great Depression**

- **The rise and decline of the Ku Klux Klan between 1915 and 1929**

The boom years

Isolationism

In 1918 the USA was the richest and most powerful country on Earth. Woodrow Wilson was President. He belonged to the Democratic Party. He had been elected in 1912 and re-elected in 1916. He had taken the USA into the First World War, helped to found the League of Nations, and wanted the USA to play a leading part in world politics.

The other main party was called the Republicans. They disagreed with Wilson.

> **Source**

A typical Republican supporter, portrayed in a novel, said,

'What the country needs ... is [not] a lot of monkeying about with foreign affairs, but a good, sound, economical business administration that will give us a chance to have something like a decent turnover.'

Sinclair Lewis: *Babbitt* (1922)

Specimen question

Who and what was Babbitt probably thinking of when he talked about 'monkeying about with foreign affairs'? [3 marks]

Republicans win control

In the 1918 elections the Republicans won control of the Senate and the House of Representatives. They reversed Wilson's policy. They refused to confirm the Treaty of Versailles and would not allow the USA to join the League of Nations. In 1920 the American people approved this policy by electing a Republican president.

The vast majority of the US population were either immigrants themselves or descended from immigrants. Between 1900 and 1915 over 13 million had landed. But after 1918 there was no shortage of labour in the USA. So in 1924 and 1929 Congress passed two Acts limiting the number of immigrants to 150,000 a year.

> **Source**

'Give me your tired, your poor,
Your huddled masses yearning to breathe free ...
Send these, the homeless, tempest-tost to me.'

Emma Lazarus: Inscription on the Statue of Liberty, 1903

Specimen question

Why in 1929 might most of the world's people feel that the US government had betrayed them? [3 marks]

Business America

Calvin Coolidge, President of the USA from 1923 to 1929, said *'the business of America is business'*. The US government helped business in various ways (*see* table).

GOVERNMENT → BUSINESS	
IMPORTS	Imports taxed
BUSINESSES	New businesses subsidised
SERVICES	Privatised, e.g. Mail
UNIONS	Weakened – strikes broken Laws
WORK	Hours de-regulated
TAXES	Incomes reduced Profits reduced

Specimen question

Study the table. How would American businesses have benefited from these policies? [8 marks]

Mass production

American businessmen, using mass production methods developed by Henry Ford to manufacture their goods, and hire purchase to sell them, set to work.

Source A

In his novels, Sinclair Lewis wrote about the businessmen at the time.

'[Everyone] in the city was hustling for hustling's sake. Men in motors were hustling to pass one another in hustling traffic . . . Men were hustling . . . to gallop across the pavement, to hurl themselves into the buildings, into hustling express elevators . . . Men who had made five thousand the year before last and ten thousand last year, were urging on nerve-yelping bodies and parched brains so that they might make twenty thousand this year.'

Sinclair Lewis: *Babbitt* (1922)

Source B

'We are a happy people – the statistics prove it. We have more cars, more bath tubs, oil furnaces, silk stockings, bank accounts than any other people on earth.'

Herbert Hoover, US President 1929–33: Speech, 1929

Source C

Table 1 Rise in income 1923–9 (%)			
	Workers' pay	Company profits	Shareholders' dividends
1923	100	100	100
1929	111	162	165

Note: This table shows the percentage rise in workers' pay, company profits and shareholders' dividends between 1923 and 1929. Workers' pay had gone up 11 per cent, profits 62 per cent and dividends 65 per cent.

Table 2				
	Surfaced roads (km)	Telephones	Radios	Cars
1919	620,000	13 million	60,000	9 million
1929	1 million	20 million	10 million	26 million

Specimen question

1 In Source A, Sinclair Lewis writes of businessmen 'hustling'. Did he approve of this? Explain your answer. **[4 marks]**

Hints

Why did Lewis think people were hustling? What effect did he think it would have on them?

Model answer

Sinclair Lewis disapproved of hustling businessmen. He thought hustling was pointless, 'hustling for hustling's sake', or that its aim was only to increase the businessmen's income, in spite of the damage it was likely to do to their health – 'nerve-yelping bodies and parched brains'.

Specimen questions

2 Read Sources B and C. Would President Hoover have agreed with Lewis? Explain your answer. How might he have used the statistics in Source C to justify his view? **[4 marks]**

3 Why might the figures in Table 1 have encouraged workers to buy shares in US companies? **[3 marks]**

Check

That you understand how the USA turned its back on the world and concentrated on making money.

American high society

Source A

'On weekends his Rolls Royce became an omnibus, bearing parties to and from the city between nine in the morning and long past midnight . . . Every Friday five crates of oranges and lemons arrived from a fruiterer in New York . . . By seven o'clock the orchestra has arrived, no thin five piece affair, but a whole pitful . . . The cars from New York are parked five deep in the drive, and already the halls and salons and verandas are gaudy with primary colours and hair bobbed in strange new ways.'

F Scott Fitzgerald: *The Great Gatsby* (a novel) (1926)

Source B

'F Scott Fitzgerald's brittle, brilliant novels of the "jazz age" caught the flavour of contemporary life perfectly.'

R B Nye and J E Morpurgo: *A History of the United States* (1955)

Specimen questions

1   Why would Source A (page 45) be useful to historians studying social life in the USA in the 1920s?   [4 marks]

2   What conclusions might they draw from it about the life led by the rich?   [6 marks]

Farmers

Compared with businessmen, American farmers were not so well off. Their standard of living was worse in the 1920s than in the war.

Notes

After the war the US government put duties on imports. This meant that other countries were unable or unwilling to buy food from the USA. So farmers could not export their produce and were worse off because they lost a lot of their former income.

Source A

US farm prices: 1919–28		
	Cotton (ccnts per lb)	Wheat ($ per bushel)
1919	35	2.20
1922	23	1.00
1925	20	1.40
1928	18	1.00

Source B

'For three quarters of a century Southern tenant farmers, white and black, had been very sad citizens, the victims of worn-out crops, living off a diet of corn, fat back pork, and no green vegetables … They were exhausted from the twin diseases of malnutrition: scurvy and pellagra.'

Alistair Cooke: *America* (1973)

Specimen questions

1   What evidence is there in Source A that farmers in the USA did not share the general prosperity of the country? [3 marks]

2   What evidence is there in Sources A and B that Southern farmers were particularly badly off?   [4 marks]

Hint

Remember that cotton was a staple crop of many Southern states.

Check

That you understand how unequal American society was.

Prohibition

In 1919 the US government prohibited the manufacture and sale of alcohol throughout the country. Why did they do this and what were the results?

Why Prohibition happened

Source A

'The drinking habits of most of my patrons appeared frightful … intoxication to the point of senselessness – and this not once in a while but frequently or daily … My unmarried patrons spent about 75% of their earnings on drink.'

New York saloon keeper: *McClure's Magazine* (1908)

Source B

Daddy's in There---

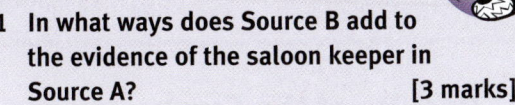

And Our Shoes and Stockings and Clothes and Food Are in There, Too, and They'll Never Come Out.
—*Chicago American.*

This cartoon was published in *Chicago America* at the beginning of the twentieth century

Source A

'You can find stills in practically every other home. They make it, they drink it, they sell it . . . You see children drunk. I have seen them drunk myself.'

Evidence from a Pennsylvania priest to a Senate committee

Source B

'There are more than 30,000 speakeasies [illegal drinking places] in New York compared with fewer than 15,000 saloons before Prohibition. They are a terrible menace . . . Fights are common in them, provoked by the raw liquor they sell and the unavoidable absence of police supervision.'

Judge Tally of New York, 1926

Source C

New York City deaths from alcoholic poisoning	
1920	98
1925	687
1926	760

Specimen questions

1 In what ways does Source B add to the evidence of the saloon keeper in Source A? **[3 marks]**

2 Why might Sources A and B persuade people that Prohibition would be a good thing? **[5 marks]**

Hint

Waste of time and money? Damage to health and family life? Remember to refer to the sources in your answer.

Prohibition in action

During Prohibition it was easy to make money manufacturing and selling illegal drink. Distillers of poor quality 'hooch' used cheap ingredients and charged high prices. And they paid no taxes. High profits attracted gangsters to the trade. The most famous, Al Capone, wiped out all his rivals and got control of the drink trade in the whole of Chicago. He made a fortune of $27 million.

In 1933 Prohibition was abolished.

Specimen question

How might an opponent of Prohibition have used the career of Al Capone and the information in Sources A, B and C to argue that it should be abolished? **[10 marks]**

Hints

How did Al Capone make his money? What evidence was there that Prohibition was turning ordinary families into criminals? Was drink more difficult to get than before? Was drinking better controlled? How was Prohibition affecting public health? Remember to back up your answer by referring to the sources.

Check

That you understand why the US government introduced Prohibition and why they reversed the ban in 1933.

The Wall Street Crash

Tip

Beware!

Share trading can be complex and technical. This explanation tries to keep it simple. Work your way through it carefully.

How the Crash happened

Between 1921 and 1929 the price of shares traded on the New York stock exchange in Wall Street rose (*see* the graph).

Buying shares seemed an easy way to make money. People borrowed money to buy shares. When the time came to pay it back, they sold the shares, which had gone up in price, and used the profit they had made to buy more shares. The fact that so many people wanted to buy shares pushed their prices even higher.

Eventually, in October 1929, some dealers decided that prices were too high. So they sold their shares. Other dealers were unwilling to buy them, so their price fell. Almost everybody now wanted to sell their shares before the price fell even further. As a result prices fell faster than ever.

On 'Black Thursday' 24 October, nearly 13 million shares were sold, and $4 million were lost. On 'Black Tuesday' 29 October more than 16 million shares were sold and the losses totalled more than $10 million. People lost their faith in shares, so they continued to fall in value.

Source

Specimen questions

Study the source.

1   **What date do you think the photograph was taken? Explain your answer.   [3 marks]**

2   **Explain how the man in the photograph might have got into the position where he had to try to sell his car for $100.**

[5 marks]

Results of the Crash

People who had borrowed money to buy shares could not pay it back when the shares lost their value. They went bankrupt. So did some of the banks which had lent them money. Other banks had less to lend.

The shortage of money affected everybody. They bought less. Factories produced less, and laid off workers. The workers bought even less, affecting other factories. The whole economy ran down (*see* the diagram on page 49).

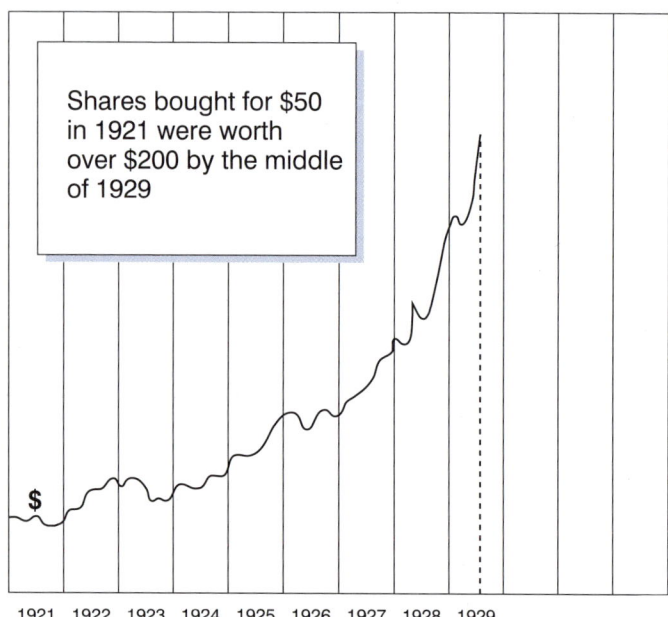

Shares bought for $50 in 1921 were worth over $200 by the middle of 1929

$

1921 1922 1923 1924 1925 1926 1927 1928 1929

US stockmarket prices

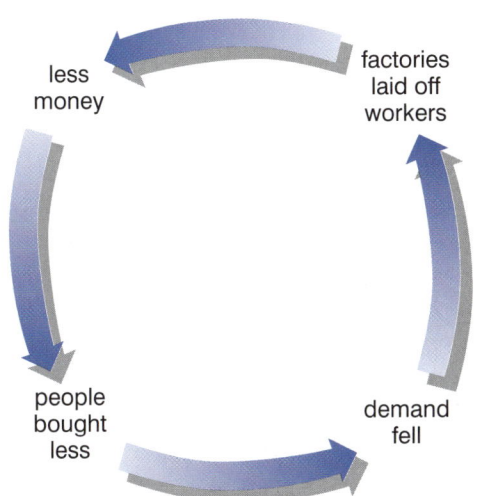

less money → factories laid off workers → demand fell → people bought less → less money

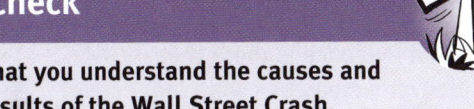

Check

That you understand the causes and results of the Wall Street Crash.

The Great Depression

The Wall Street Crash was followed by a slump in trade and industry which was so deep and so long lasting that it became known as the Great Depression.

Causes of the Depression

The most obvious cause of the Depression was the Wall Street Crash. But there were others such as depressed agriculture, low wages, credit excess and production excess.

Specimen question

Do you agree that the main cause of the Depression was the Wall Street Crash? Explain your answer fully.   [15 marks]

Hints

Faced with a question like this, you have to decide what to put in, what to leave out and how to organise your answer. A couple of general rules:

1   You will not get good marks by discussing only the cause mentioned in the question. You need to deal with others as well.

2   Keep checking to make sure that you are answering the question. You get no credit for information, however accurate, that has nothing to do with the actual question.

Model answer

The American Depression was caused by a number of factors. The boom had to come to an end sooner or later. For one thing, by 1929 American factories were producing more than they could sell. So they would have had to cut production and lay off workers anyway. In addition, too much of the trade depended on borrowed money. Consumers used hire purchase to buy cars and household goods, and people who bought shares borrowed money to pay for them. Many owed more than they could afford to pay back, and so could not afford to buy more. So for this reason too, trade inevitably slowed down.

What was more, most Americans were not earning enough to keep the boom going. Farmers' incomes were less than in 1919, and workers' wages had not increased very much. So the boom was bound to end, even without the Crash. But the Crash made the Depression much worse than it need have been. It happened so suddenly that people had no time to adjust. Many people lost so much so quickly that they felt helpless. So the Wall Street Crash was not the main reason that the Depression happened, but it did make it worse.

Check

That you understand why the Depression happened.

The effects of the Depression

Source A

Economic statistics showing percentage change between 1929 and 1932		
	1929	1932
Share prices	100	17
Overall production	100	60
Wages	100	40
Share dividends	100	43
Foreign trade	100	30
Unemployment	100	600

Source B

'Eleven hundred men standing in a Salvation Army breadline on March 10 1930 near the Bowey Hotel in Manhattan, descended upon two trucks delivering baked goods to the hotel . . . Cookies, rolls and bread were flung into the street with the hungry jobless chasing after them.'

Irving Bernstein: *The Lean Years* (1960)

Source C

'Eleven children in that house. They've got no shoes, no pants. In the house, no chairs. My God, you go in there, you cry, that's all.'

A Philadelphia shopkeeper reported in *The Nation* (1932)

Source D

'I couldn't go out in the evening to mail a letter without being stopped by nicely dressed men who had told their wives they were out looking for night work. So they were – they were out on the streets cadging dimes and quarters.'

Alistair Cooke, writing of the early 1930s: *America* (1973)

Specimen question

Study the sources. What evidence do they offer that:

(a) by 1932 American trade and industry had seriously declined

(b) the Depression had hit most classes of people in the USA

(c) in some places there was real want and a mood of despair

(d) law and order were threatened by the Depression? **[15 marks]**

Hoover and the Depression

President Hoover (1929–33) did not think the government could do much to end the Depression. He thought the country would have to wait until business recovered of its own accord. But he did do a little:

1. The Reconstruction Finance Corporation (RFC) provided loans to banks, farmers and industrialists.
2. Increased tariffs were intended to make imports more expensive and so encourage people to buy American goods.
3. Taxes were reduced to encourage people to spend.
4. Food relief in the form of soup and bread was provided.

Source A

'In Hoover we trusted, now we are busted'
Banner carried by unemployed workers
'Hoovervilles'
Name given to shanty towns built and inhabited by the homeless

Source B

'The Country needs . . . and demands bold, persistent experimentation . . . Above all, try something.'
F Roosevelt: Campaign speech, 1932

Specimen question

1. What evidence is there that Hoover's measures were ineffective?
   [5 marks]

Hint

Use your knowledge as well as the sources.

Specimen question

2. What evidence is there that many people blamed Hoover for the situation? Would he have thought this fair? Explain your answer. **[8 marks]**

Hint

To answer this question you need to point out what Hoover did to try to improve the situation, as well as dealing with his views on the helplessness of the government.

Specimen question

3. Why in 1932 would people be more likely to vote for Roosevelt than for Hoover? **[3 marks]**

The New Deal

Roosevelt's policies

Franklin Roosevelt was elected President in November 1932. He took over in March 1933 and set to work at once.

Roosevelt used many ideas to try to solve America's problems. If an idea worked, he persisted with it. If it did not, he dropped it and tried something else. He never gave up.

He tried so many different schemes it is difficult to keep track of them all.

Source A

'First of all let me assert my firm belief that the only thing we have to fear is fear itself . . . Our greatest primary task is to put people to work . . . It can be accomplished in part by direct recruiting by the government itself, treating the task as we would the emergency of a war but at the same time . . . accomplishing greatly needed projects.'

President Roosevelt: Inaugural address, 1933

Source B

'In other periods of depression it has always been possible to see some things which were solid and on which you could base hope, but as I look about, I now see nothing to give ground for hope.'

Ex-President Coolidge: Speech, 1933

Specimen questions

1 **What was the main difference between Coolidge's attitude to the Depression and that of Roosevelt? Explain your answer.** [5 marks]

2 **Study the diagram on the right. How did the CCC, the TVA, the EHS and the WPA help to 'put people to work' and accomplish 'greatly needed projects'?** [10 marks]

Notes

AAA	Agricultural Adjustment Act
CCC	Civilian Conservation Corps
EHS	Emergency Housing Section
FLSA	Fair Labour Standards Act
HOLC	Home Owners Loan Corporation
NRA	National Recovery Administration
SSA	Social Security Act
TVA	Tennessee Valley Authority
WPA	Works Progress Administration

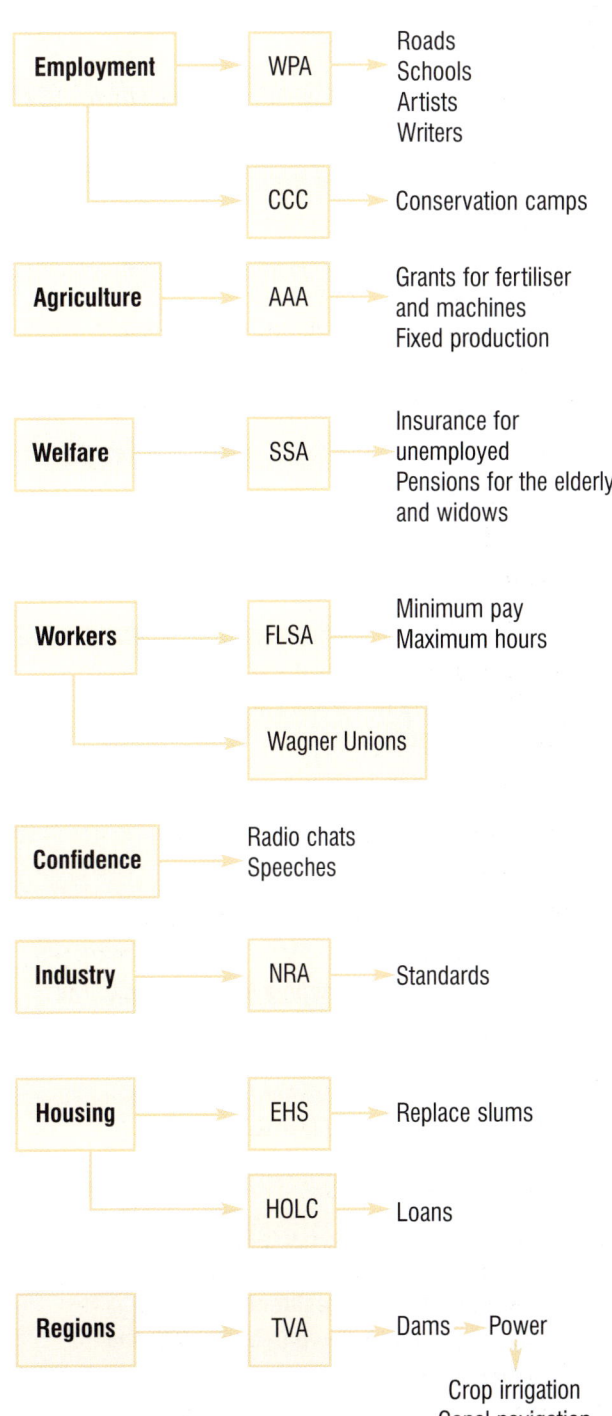

Employment → WPA → Roads, Schools, Artists, Writers

→ CCC → Conservation camps

Agriculture → AAA → Grants for fertiliser and machines, Fixed production

Welfare → SSA → Insurance for unemployed, Pensions for the elderly and widows

Workers → FLSA → Minimum pay, Maximum hours

→ Wagner Unions

Confidence → Radio chats, Speeches

Industry → NRA → Standards

Housing → EHS → Replace slums

→ HOLC → Loans

Regions → TVA → Dams → Power → Crop irrigation, Canal navigation, Industry

Roosevelt and the people

Source A

A cartoon published in the *New York Daily News* in 1933

Source B

'They missed the way the President used to talk to them. They'd say, "He used to talk to me about my government". There was a real dialogue between Franklin and the people.'

Reaction of people to Roosevelt's death, described by Mrs Roosevelt: *When FDR died* (1961)

Source C

Dear Mr President,

'This is just to tell you everything is all right now. The man you sent found our house all right and we went down to the bank with him and the mortgage can go on for a while longer . . . I never heard of a President like you, Mr Roosevelt . . . God bless you.'

Letter sent to President Roosevelt in 1936

Specimen questions

1 What means did President Roosevelt use to keep in touch with the American people? **[2 marks]**

2 What evidence is there that he was successful? **[4 marks]**

Hint

Look at all three sources.

Specimen questions

3 What agency, do you think, had helped the man who wrote Source C? Explain your answer. **[4 marks]**

4 Study the diagram on page 51. What schemes did President Roosevelt introduce to improve life for ordinary people? **[6 marks]**

5 In April 1936 *Time* magazine wrote, 'Today, with few exceptions, members of the so-called Upper Class frankly hate Franklin Roosevelt'. Why was this? **[10 marks]**

Hints

Roosevelt increased taxes to pay for his reforms. Roosevelt increased the power of the trade unions. Roosevelt tried to control big business. Roosevelt took power into his own hands.

Check

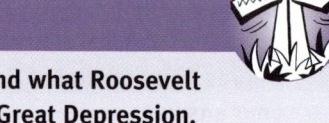

That you understand what Roosevelt did to counter the Great Depression.

The results of the New Deal

Source A

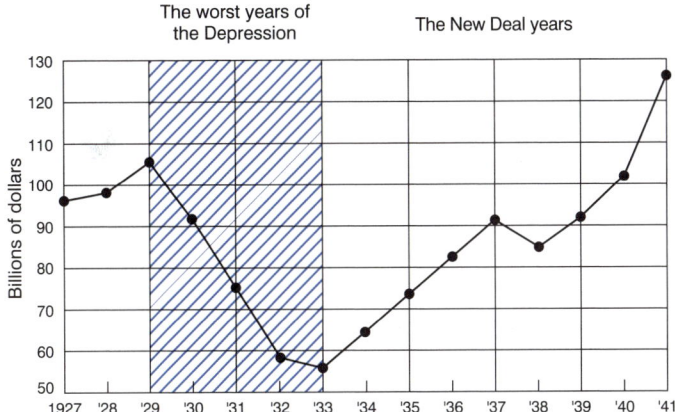

The worst years of the Depression

The New Deal years

The Gross National Product of the USA 1927–41
(1929 prices)

Source B

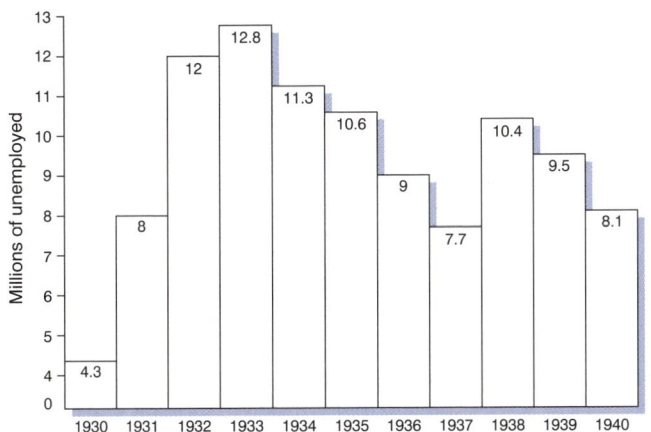

Unemployment in the USA 1930–40

Specimen question

'The New Deal was successful in solving the economic problems of the Depression in the USA.' Do you agree? Explain your answer fully. [15 marks]

Hints

As usual in questions like this, the safest answer is one which agrees up to a point.

Notice that the question asks only about economic problems. So writing a lot about, for instance, social security and housing will get you few, if any, marks.

Remember that there is no right or wrong answer to this question. The examiners want to see if you can say what you think, and back it up with evidence.

A good way to approach the question would be:

1 to point out that, according to the sources, by 1940:
   (a) Gross National Product (GNP) had recovered to near that in 1930
   (b) unemployment had fallen, but not to the level of 1930
   so the economic problems seem to have been at least partly solved

2 to say that, even without the New Deal, the USA economy would probably have picked up in any case

3 to point out that the quickest recovery in GNP and employment happened after the outbreak of war in 1939 when the USA was increasing production to help in the war against Germany

4 to conclude that the impact of the New Deal was limited. But it gave people confidence and at least helped the economy to pick up more quickly than it would have otherwise.

Check

That you know how far the New Deal was a success.

The Ku Klux Klan

The Klan was a racist organisation founded in the Southern states of the USA in 1865 to prevent black Americans being treated as equal to whites. It was revived in 1915, targeting Jews and Roman Catholics as well as blacks.

Many traditionalists feared that the outsiders would bring in new races, different religions, trade unions and strikes, and so destroy their traditional way of life. So they joined the Klan to keep the newcomers 'in their place' and, if possible, drive them out.

In 1921 Congress investigated the Klan and found it guilty of violence, immorality and corruption. For a time it concentrated on political activity. Many Americans approved of its aims and, as long as it seemed respectable, joined it, so that its membership reached almost 3 million in 1924. Membership had decreased to 10,000 by 1929.

But the Klan's leaders quarrelled among themselves and there were strong rumours of immorality and more stories of violence. So opposition to the Klan increased, while at the same time the country's growing prosperity quietened the fears of many of its supporters. So it lost members, though it was never disbanded.

Notes

- Between 1915 and 1918, at least 199 black Americans were lynched.
- Between 1919 and 1922, 239 more were killed.
- In 1919 a race riot in Chicago lasted thirteen days: 15 whites and 23 blacks were killed.

Specimen question

Why did the Ku Klux Klan grow so quickly between 1915 and 1924, and then decline in numbers so suddenly? [15 marks]

Model answer

Between 1914 and 1929 American industry boomed, while after 1919 agriculture was less prosperous. Agricultural workers thought they would be better off working in industrial towns than in the countryside. So they moved in. Many were blacks from the Southern states. Some had fought in the war, and thought they deserved equal rights, as was the case in Europe.

Source A

'No State shall make or enforce any law which shall abridge [reduce] the privileges or immunities [rights] of citizens of the United States.'

Article 14 of the Constitution of the USA, passed in 1868

Notes

This article was intended to ensure that all citizens of the USA had equal rights. In 1892 Homer Plessey, who was black, complained that his rights were 'abridged' because in Louisiana there were separate railway carriages for white and black passengers. In 1896 the Supreme Court said that, provided the separate facilities were 'equal', they were within the law. This cleared the way, for example, for separate schools, hospitals, barracks and buses.

Source B

'The right of citizens of the United States to vote shall not be denied . . . on account of race [or] color.'

Article 15 of the Constitution of the USA, passed in 1870

Source C

'Mississippi adopted a poll tax and a literacy test as requirements for voters in 1890, and by 1910 every southern state had adopted some [such] type of scheme. These provisions eliminated virtually all Afro-Americans from the voting lists.'

Kenneth C Goode: *From Africa to the United States* (1969)

Specimen questions

1 Explain why Source B did not make the schemes described in Source C illegal. [4 marks]

2 Using the sources and your own knowledge, explain why many black Americans felt they were denied their rights as US citizens. [10 marks]

Check

That you understand the reasons for the rise and decline of the Ku Klux Klan.

Preview

What you need to know:

- **How the Germans defeated Allied armies in the early months**
- **How the Luftwaffe tried to win control of the air over England**
- **How Hitler attempted to conquer the USSR**
- **How the German navy tried to get and keep control of the Atlantic**
- **The war between the USA and Japan in the Far East**
- **How the two sides used bombers in the war in Europe**
- **How the Second World War affected life in Britain**

The Blitzkrieg 1939–40

The German generals decided to use a new system of war called *'Blitzkrieg'* (lightning war), in which dive-bombers suddenly attacked enemy roads, railways and airfields while tanks and motorised infantry advanced as fast as they could. By the time the defenders realised what was happening, it was too late.

Blitzkrieg timeline

Sept 1939	German and Soviet troops overran Poland.
April 1940	Germany occupied Denmark and Norway.
May 1940	Germany invaded Holland, Belgium and France.
June 1940	France surrendered.

Notes

- The Germans did not attack between the end of September 1939 and April 1940 because they had used up all their supplies of fuel and ammunition in defeating Poland.
- The French had not bothered to fortify the Ardennes, where the Germans broke through (*see* map), because they thought the country was too rough for an invading army to cross.

Source A

'When we have devoted so much effort to building up a fortified barrier [the Maginot Line], do you imagine that we would be mad enough to go out in front of this barrier into all sorts of danger?'

French Minister of War in a speech to the National Assembly

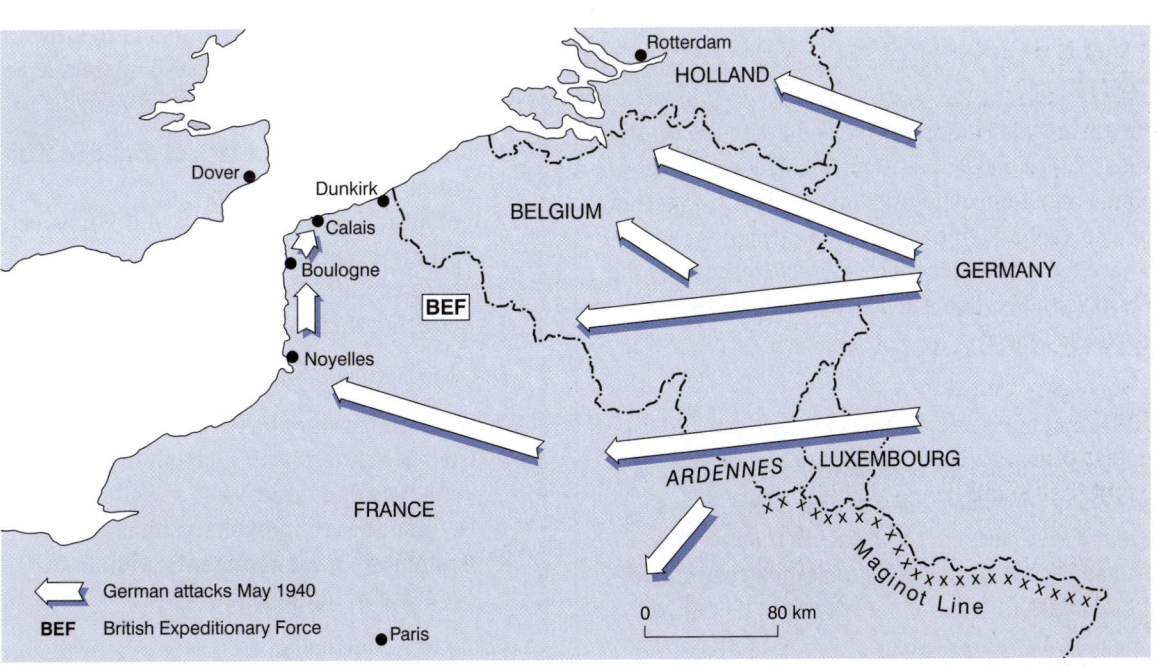

German attacks in May 1940

German attacks May 1940
BEF   British Expeditionary Force   •Paris

0   80 km

The Second World War

Source B

'The [German] thrust could have been stopped . . . by a concentrated counterstroke with similar forces. But the French, though having more and better tanks than the enemy, had strung them out in small packets in the 1918 way.'

B Liddell Hart, a British General: *Memoirs* (1965)

Specimen question

Study Sources A and B. Were the French prepared for war in 1940? Explain your answer. [4 marks]

Hint

Like many questions in History, there is no straightforward 'right' answer.

Model answer

In a way the French were prepared because they had built the Maginot Line and equipped their army with large numbers of modern tanks. On the other hand they were not prepared to fight an attacking war, and did not know how to use tanks effectively. So they had the right equipment and the wrong ideas.

Dunkirk

The British army in France was driven back to the coast. Between 27 May and 3 June 1940, 338,226 men were evacuated from Dunkirk to Britain. Nobody had expected so many to get back. At the time the British press and radio gave the impression that most were rescued by the owners of countless boats and small ships who sailed across to fetch them.

Source A

'All day and all night men of the undefeated British Expeditionary Force have been coming home . . . It is clear that if they have not come back in triumph they have come back in glory . . . that they know they did not meet their masters.'

BBC Radio News, 31 May 1940

Source B

'I was seven years old in 1940 . . . When I began to write this book, I struggled to substantiate the familiar belief that an armada of "little ships" played a significant part in the rescue of the army . . . I realised that this was false. The little ships operated only on the last two days of the British evacuation, and then to very little effect.'

Nicholas Harman: *Dunkirk*: *The Necessary Myth* (1980)

Specimen questions

1. Was the radio announcer telling the truth when he said the British Expeditionary Force was 'undefeated'? Explain your answer. [4 marks]

2. What reasons can you suggest to explain how the popular story of the 'little ships' came into being? [4 marks]

3. Do you believe what Nicholas Harman says about the evacuation? Explain your answer. [4 marks]

4. 'The successes of the German army in 1940 were due to Allied mistakes.' Do you agree? Explain your answer fully. [15 marks]

Hints

You can use your own knowledge as well as the sources to answer this. The safest way to tackle questions like this is to strike a balance. So, the Allies did make mistakes. For example:

1. displaying a general lack of confidence and initiative
2. not attacking the Germans while they were still restocking after invading Poland
3. not fortifying the Ardennes
4. not using their tanks effectively.

But, the Germans fought well. For example:

1. their troops were full of confidence
2. their Blitzkrieg tactics – explain them – were new and effective
3. their sudden, unprovoked attacks – give examples – gave opponents no time to organise or fight back.

Come to a conclusion.

Norway

The German attack on Norway (1940) brought about a change in the British government. Norway was important because Sweden exported iron ore to Germany through the Norwegian port of Narvik. In addition, Norway was the shortest route to get help to Finland, which was fighting against the USSR.

Norway timeline

5 February	British government approved an attack on Narvik.
13 March	Finland surrendered to the USSR.
14 March	Attack on Narvik cancelled.
26 March	Plan to attack Narvik approved again.
2 April	Chamberlain made a speech, claiming *'Hitler has missed the bus'*.
9 April	German troops overran Denmark and invaded Norway.
14–17 April	British troops landed at Namsos, Narvik and Andalsnes.
29 April	British troops landed at Bodo.
2 & 3 May	British troops evacuated from Namsos and Andalsnes.
7 & 8 May	Debate in House of Commons which forced Chamberlain to resign.

Specimen question

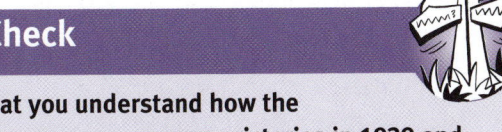

Study the timeline. What evidence is there in it of the British government's:

(a) complacency

(b) indecision and bad planning?   [5 marks]

Check

That you understand how the Germans won so many victories in 1939 and 1940.

The Battle of Britain

After the fall of France, Hitler decided to invade England (Operation Sealion). He needed the Luftwaffe to escort the invasion barges full of troops across the Channel. First he had to destroy the RAF.

Between 12 August and 7 September 1940, German bombers and fighters attacked British air bases. In this time they destroyed about 630 fighters. But they believed they had destroyed more than 3000. So Göring, head of the Luftwaffe, thought he had defeated the RAF and decided to attack London instead.

The biggest raid was on 15 September. RAF fighters shot down 60 German planes. The RAF lost 26. Göring realised that the RAF was too strong for Germany to risk invading England. Hitler cancelled his invasion plans.

Notes

- **Range**
  Fighters did not carry enough fuel to fly long distances. So the RAF had an advantage flying close to their bases.

- **Radar**
  Radar showed exactly where the German planes were. So the RAF did not have to waste time and fuel looking for them.

- **Pilots**
  Pilots whose planes were shot down in the battle often parachuted down over southern England or into the sea nearby. German pilots were picked up and imprisoned. British pilots were available to go on flying. So the RAF needed fewer replacements than the Luftwaffe.

- **Planes**
  Lord Beaverbrook was in charge of aircraft production. Britain's factories produced more planes than the Luftwaffe destroyed during the Battle of Britain. Germany's aircraft factories were badly organised.

Source A

'This switch to London from military targets, from air bases, changed the situation for Great Britain and Fighter Command considerably. If we would have continued to attack the bases perhaps the situation would have been changed.'

Adolf Galland, 1940 Luftwaffe Wing Commander: Television interview, 1973

Source B

'The attack didn't go to the airfields. It went to London. And the airfields were spared so they were able to pull themselves together, sort themselves out, repair things and, most important of the lot, give the pilots more of a chance for a little rest.'

Robert Wright, a member of Dowding's staff in 1940: Television interview, 1973

Specimen question

1   Read Sources A and B. Which of the two speakers was likely to know more about the situation in the Battle of Britain? Explain your answer.   **[4 marks]**

Hints

Galland fought in the war in the air. What would he have known about conditions on the ground? Wright was on Dowding's (head of fighter command) staff. Would he have had more complete information? Extra credit for spotting that by 1973 they might both have done research and so know about the same information.

Specimen question

2   Are Sources A and B strong evidence that the RAF would have been defeated if the Luftwaffe had continued to attack the airfields? Explain your answer.   **[10 marks]**

Hints

Remember that you can use your own knowledge of the topic as well as the sources to answer the question, and that the examiner is more interested in the way you use the evidence than in the conclusion you reach.

Does either source suggest that continuing to attack the airfields would certainly have defeated the RAF? Does either offer strong evidence that the situation was serious? Give examples.

What continuing advantages did the RAF possess? Come to a conclusion.

Check

That you understand why the RAF won the Battle of Britain.

Barbarossa – invasion of the Soviet Union

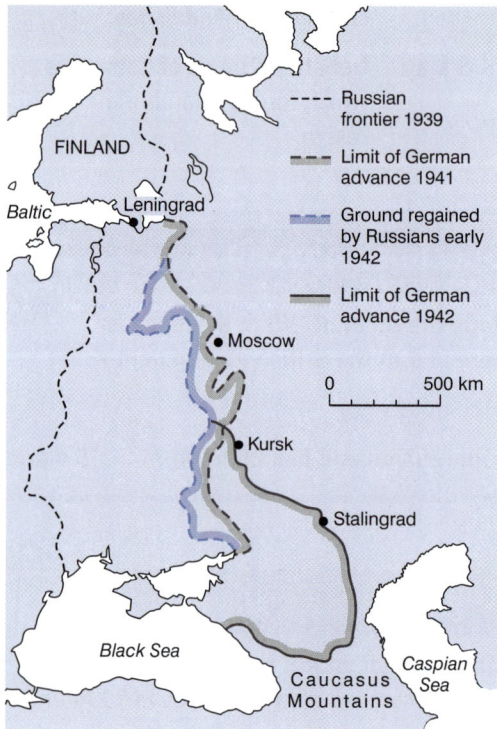

- - - -	Russian frontier 1939
– · – · –	Limit of German advance 1941
▬▬▬	Ground regained by Russians early 1942
———	Limit of German advance 1942

FINLAND

Baltic

Leningrad

Moscow

Kursk

Stalingrad

0   500 km

Black Sea

Caucasus Mountains

Caspian Sea

The Eastern Front 1939–42

In June 1941, without any warning, German troops invaded the Soviet Union.

Hitler thought it would be easy. *'We have only to kick in the door and the whole rotten structure will come crashing down,'* he told General Jodl. The map opposite shows you how far the German army penetrated into the Soviet Union.

Tip

Maps can help you to understand and remember. Try drawing your own to help with revision.

Problems for Germany

Early in the campaign there were warning signs that the invasion was not going Hitler's way.

Source A

'When the war began we had expected 200 enemy divisions. Now we have already counted 350. These divisions are certainly not properly armed and equipped as we would see it and they are often lacking in tactical leadership. But they are there. And whenever a dozen of these divisions are destroyed, the Russians replace them with another dozen.'

Franz Halder, German army Chief of Staff: *Diary* (11 August 1941)

Source B

'We had no gloves. We had no winter shoes. We had no equipment whatsoever to fight or withstand the cold . . . Due to the cold we lost a lot of people who got frost-bitten . . . As it became colder . . . most of our artillery had become completely unusable. Guns didn't fire any more.'

Ekkehard Maurer, German army officer: Television interview, 1973

Source C

'We saw [Siberian troops] after taking this small village . . . Very big men with very good winter clothes . . . And then my feeling was a very bad one, because this was the sign that the Russian people, the Russian government was able to take troops from the far east and to transport them to the front at Moscow.'

Rolf Elble, German army officer: Television interview, 1973

Specimen question

Study the sources. In what ways do they show that the Germans had underestimated the difficulties of fighting against the Soviet Union? [8 marks]

Soviet recovery

After 1941 the Soviet Union recovered. It set up vast new factories in the east and recruited new armies. So production increased, as did the size of the army.

The Soviet planners used their resources sensibly. They chose a few robust, reliable weapons and built huge numbers of them. Also Stalin, their leader, learned by his mistakes. In the first year of the war he had taken all the important military decisions himself. He was not a professional soldier and he had often been wrong. After 1942 he usually followed the advice of Marshal Georgi Zhukov, the Deputy Commissar of Defence, who understood modern warfare. Under his command, the Soviet army began to win battles.

Stalingrad timeline

July 1942	Hitler ordered a three-fold attack, on the Caucasus, Leningrad and Stalingrad.
Sept 1942	German troops entered the outskirts of Stalingrad.
8 Nov 1942	Hitler boasted: *'We've got it . . . No one will ever be able to get us out now.'*
23 Nov 1942	Soviet armies surrounded German forces in Stalingrad.
31 Jan 1943	German commander, Von Paulus, surrendered with 90,000 men.

Source A

'The Germans could not stand close fighting . . . They could not bear us to come close to them when we counter-attacked . . . We should get as close to the enemy as possible . . . Every German soldier must be made to feel he was living under the muzzle of a Russian gun.'

General Chuikov, Soviet commander of Stalingrad: *The Beginning of the Road* (1963)

Source B

'*Stalingrad is Hell on earth ... We attack every day. If we capture twenty yards in the morning, the Russians throw us back again in the evening.*'

Letter from a German NCO serving in Stalingrad

Specimen question

1   Historians agree that General Chuikov was the right man to send to command the Soviet forces in Stalingrad. Do the sources support this view? Explain your answer.   [4 marks]

Model answer

Yes, the sources do support this view because he found out that the Germans did not like hand-to-hand fighting. To exploit this he told his troops to keep as close to the Germans as possible. This proved very successful, helping to create 'a Hell on earth' for the Germans.

Specimen question

2   Why was Stalingrad a 'Hell on earth' for the German troops?   [8 marks]

Hints

You are *not* tied to the sources in this question. You can use your own knowledge of the topic as well. There is not one, full, correct answer. The examiners will be looking for perhaps six relevant points, backed up with examples.

You might mention: cold, hunger, lack of supplies, fear of the enemy, poor medical facilities, distance from home, unfamiliar battle tactics (e.g. remember they were trained for Blitzkrieg, not hand-to-hand fighting), desolation of their surroundings, gradually increasing sense of hopelessness.

Hitler's leadership

Source A

'*[Hitler] had his own picture of the world and every fact had to be fitted into that personal picture ... But in fact it was a picture of another world.*'

General Guderian, Hitler's Chief of Staff 1944–45: *Panzer Leader* (1952)

Source B

'*When a statement was read to him which showed that Stalin would be able to muster another ... million men north of Stalingrad ... Hitler flew at the man who was reading with clenched fists and foam in the corners of his mouth and forbade him to read such idiotic twaddle.*'

Franz Halder, Hitler's army Chief of Staff 1938–42: *Hitler as Warlord* (1950)

Source C

'*Our enemies rightly regarded this disaster at Stalingrad as a turning point in the war. But at Hitler's headquarters the only reaction was a temporary numbness.*'

Albert Speer, Hitler's armaments minister: *Inside the Third Reich* (1970)

Specimen questions

1   Study the sources. Do Sources B and C confirm Guderian's view of how Hitler's mind worked? Explain your answer.   [5 marks]

2   Do you think the information contained in these sources is reliable? Explain your answer.   [4 marks]

Hints

Were the authors in a position to know? Do they tell the same story? Had they any motive for lying?

Soviet victory

Source A

Source A

A cartoon published in the Soviet Union in 1942

Specimen question

1 Was the cartoon an accurate representation of the situation in 1942? Explain your answer. [5 marks]

Hints

Strength of Hitler? Part played by the USA and Britain in 1942?

Specimen question

2 Why, do you think, did the Soviet government publish the cartoon in 1942? [3 marks]

Source B

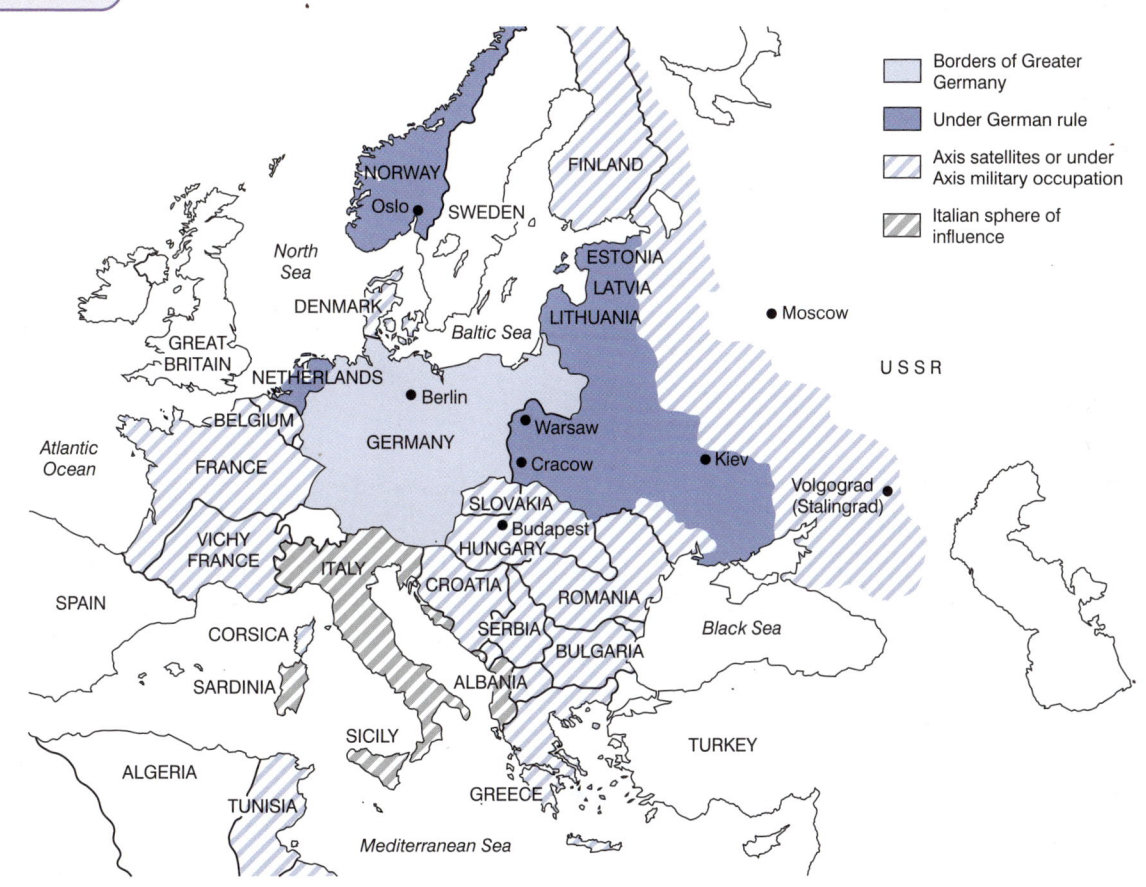

Borders of Greater Germany

Under German rule

Axis satellites or under Axis military occupation

Italian sphere of influence

Germany's expansion through Europe 1942

The Soviet advance

In July 1943 there was a huge battle at Kursk, where the Germans lost 2700 tanks and 900,000 men. They were now much weaker than the Soviets (*see* the table).

German and Soviet military strength 1943		
	Men	**Tanks**
German	2.5 million	2,300
Soviets	5.5 million	8,400

The Soviet army advanced steadily (*see* map). The Russian war ended in May 1945 when Soviet troops captured Berlin. The Soviet Union had defeated Hitler, but in so doing had lost 20 million people.

People in Britain and the USA have often not given enough credit to the part played by the Soviet Union in the defeat of Germany. They have concentrated instead on the campaigns fought by British and American troops in North Africa and Italy, and on the invasion of Northern France in 1944. But in 1945 only 35 German divisions were fighting against British and American troops. More than 200 were fighting the Soviet army in the east.

Specimen question

Why was the part played by the Soviet Union in the war neglected by people in Britain and the USA? [5 marks]

Hints

Cold War? Patriotism?

Check

That you understand how and why the Soviet Union defeated the Germans.

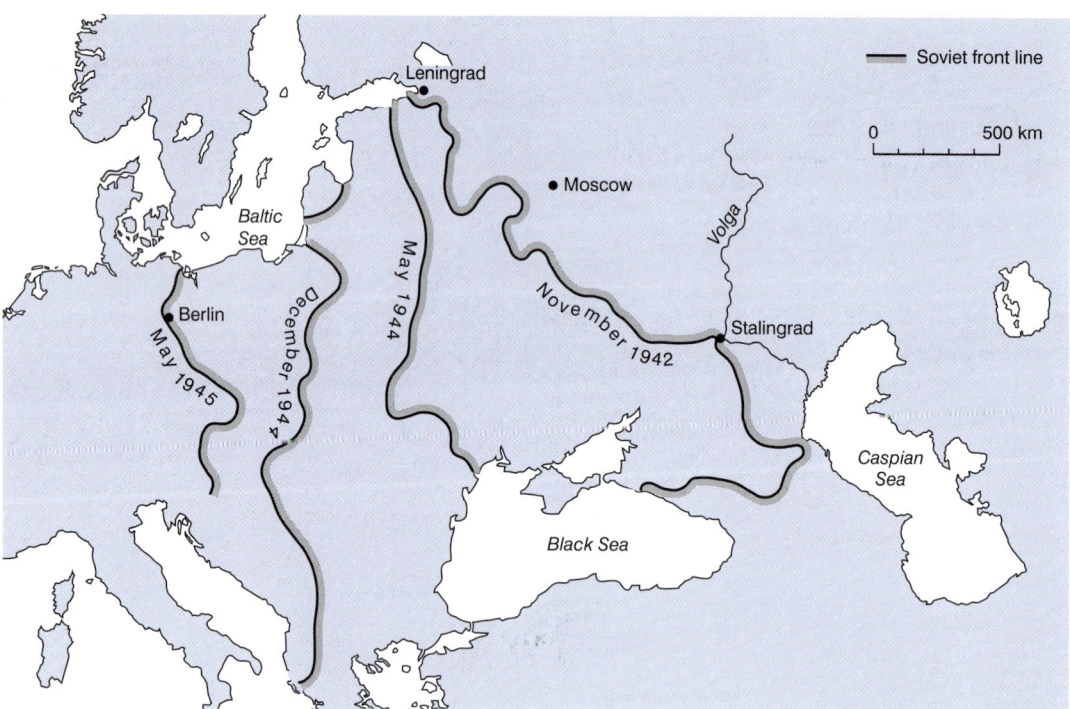

Soviet front line 1942–45

The Battle of the Atlantic

The most important sea battle of the war was fought by German U-boats trying to prevent supplies crossing the Atlantic to Britain. Merchant ships were grouped together into convoys escorted by warships and aircraft. The U-boats attacked them in the 'Mid-Atlantic Gap' while they were out of range of aircraft based on land.

In 1942, U-boats sank 5.4 million tons of Allied shipping, and reduced Britain's imports to a third of what they had been in 1939. But during 1943 the number of U-boats destroyed increased (*see* table). Look at the notes that follow to understand why this happened.

U-boats destroyed	
Mar 1943	15
Apr 1943	19
May 1943	41

Notes

- **Intelligence**
  The Admiralty was able to tell the convoys where the U-boats were likely to be.

- **Training**
  The navy and air force improved the training of the crews of ships and planes escorting the convoys.

- **Technology**
  VLR (Very Long Range) aircraft could 'cover' more of the ocean.
  Planes carried Leigh lights, which could light up U-boats on the surface at night.
  New radar enabled aircraft to spot U-boats on the surface more easily.

- **Portugal**
  In October 1943 Portugal allowed the Allies to use an air base on the Azores. This closed the Mid-Atlantic Gap.

Source A

'The submarine will in the end decide the outcome of the war.'
Hitler, June 1942

Source B

'The only peril that ever frightened me during the war was the U-boat peril.'
Winston Churchill: *The Second World War* (1950)

Source C

'Enemy aircraft have been equipped with a new location apparatus . . . which enables them to detect submarines and to attack them unexpectedly in low cloud, bad visibility or at night . . . Losses have risen from 14 submarines, that is about 13% of those at sea, to 36 submarines, or perhaps 37, that is about 30% of the submarines at sea. These losses are too high.'
Admiral Dönitz: Memorandum to Hitler, May 1943

Specimen questions

1 In May 1943 Dönitz withdrew the U-boats from the North Atlantic. What would (a) Hitler and (b) Churchill have thought of this? Explain your answer.
[4 marks]

2 Dönitz mentions only one reason for growing U-boat losses. Why, do you think, did he not mention the others? [4 marks]

3 Why was Dönitz careful to quote exact numbers in his memorandum? [4 marks]

Hint

Look at Source A. Would it be easy to persuade Hitler to withdraw the U-boats?

Merchant seamen

Source

'More than 32,000 died at sea during World War II, all of them volunteers, out of a total of about 145,000. The overall casualty rate in the British Merchant Navy during World War II was higher than that in any of the armed services . . . British Merchant seamen were never actually compelled to sign on for another voyage . . . These civilians went back to sea again time after time simply because they were sailors and thought they should.'
Mark Arnold-Forster: *The World at War* (1973)

1 How does the writer try to make the reader share his admiration for merchant seamen?   [3 marks]

2 Does the fact that the writer admires merchant seamen make the figures he quotes unreliable? Explain your answer.

[4 marks]

Check

That you understand how important the war in the Atlantic was, and how the Allies won it.

The Pacific war

Outbreak

After 1900 Japan's industry developed rapidly, but she needed raw materials and overseas markets to sell what she produced. She needed an empire, but most of the territories in the area belonged to other countries. The Japanese realised that they might have to fight for what they wanted, so they built up their armed forces.

Japanese expansion timeline

1910		Japan annexed Korea.
1914		Japan took over Germany's Pacific colonies.
1931		Japan invaded Manchuria.
1933		Japan left the League of Nations.
1941	July	Japan occupied French Indo-China. USA banned oil exports to Japan (90 per cent of Japan's oil).
	Dec	Japan attacked Pearl Harbor. Sank fourteen US warships. Destroyed more than 300 aircraft. 3500 US casualties. USA and Britain declared war on Japan. Germany declared war on the USA.

Specimen questions

1 How could the USA have justified their refusal to sell oil to Japan?   [4 marks]

2 How could Japan have justified their attack on Pearl Harbor?   [4 marks]

Tip

Remember, mini timelines are a compact way of presenting information. Try compiling your own to help with your revision.

Japanese victories

After Pearl Harbor, Japanese armies quickly overran much of the Pacific (*see* map opposite). The Japanese were able to take over so much land so quickly mainly because they were well prepared with ships, planes and equipment, their men were trained and motivated, and because their enemies were complacent.

Japanese victories timeline

Dec 1941	Invaded Malaya, captured Guam, Wake, Hong Kong.
Feb 1942	Captured Singapore.
Mar 1942	Conquered the Dutch East Indies.
April 1942	Conquered Burma.
May 1942	Conquered the Philippines.

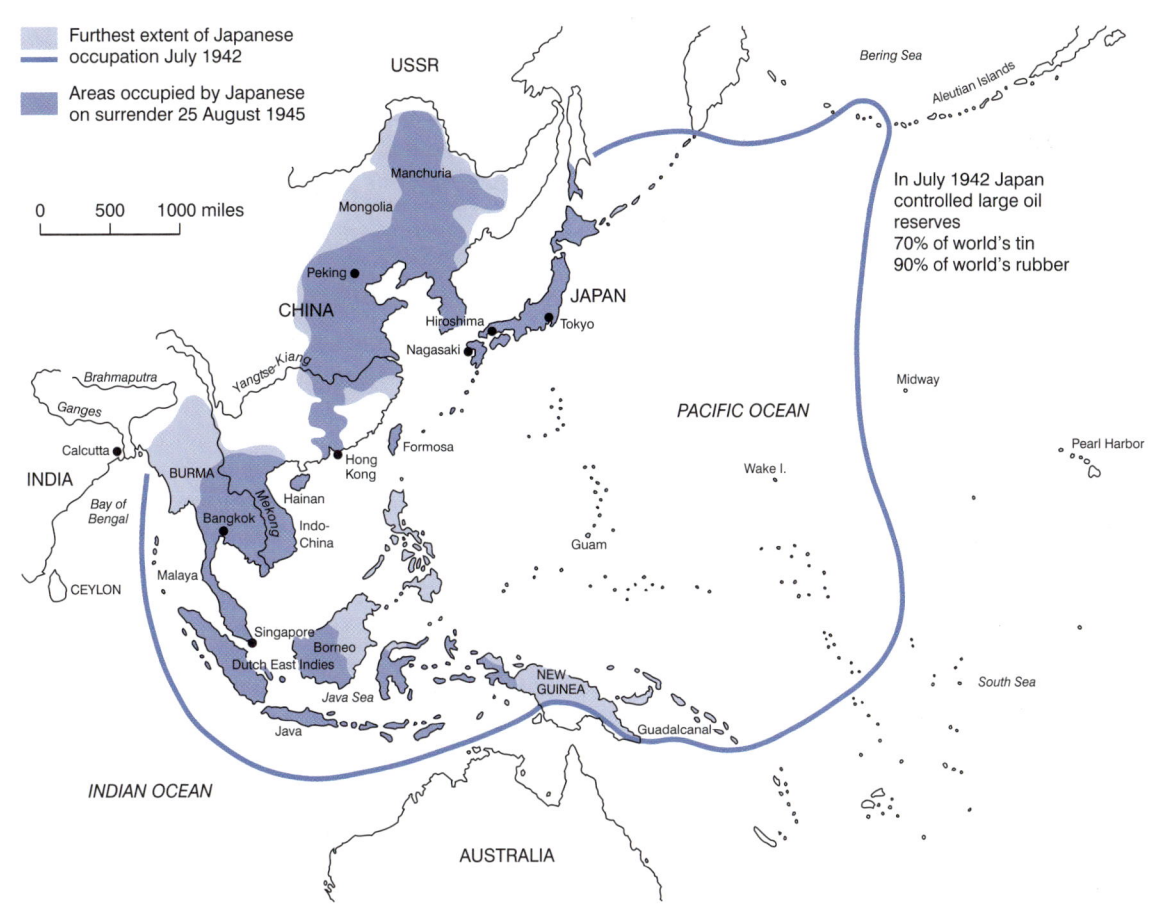

Furthest extent of Japanese occupation July 1942

Areas occupied by Japanese on surrender 25 August 1945

0   500   1000 miles

In July 1942 Japan controlled large oil reserves
70% of world's tin
90% of world's rubber

The USA counter-attack

In the Pacific war, control of the sea was vital to protect the ships carrying troops and supplies to the islands. The most important warships were aircraft carriers, whose planes could bomb and sink enemy battleships. When the Japanese attacked Pearl Harbor, the US navy's four largest aircraft carriers were out at sea and so were safe.

In June 1942 the Japanese decided to capture Midway Island. The US navy broke Japanese codes and were waiting for them. In 10 minutes US planes sank four Japanese aircraft carriers and killed or injured 240 of Japan's best pilots.

> **Source**
>
> 'After Midway I was certain there was no chance of success.'
>
> Mitsumasa Yonai, Japanese Navy Minister, when interrogated after the war

> **Specimen question**
>
> **Why, do you think, did the Battle of Midway convince Mitsumasa Yonai that Japan could not win the war?** [3 marks]

The A bombs

The USA began to recapture the islands taken by Japan. And when they were close enough they began to bomb Japan itself. In August 1945 they dropped two atom bombs, one on Hiroshima and one on Nagasaki. Japan surrendered.

> **Source A**
>
> 'The Japanese were tough fighters. They never would give up ... We tried to persuade the Japanese to surrender. But they kept fighting ... and we soldiers had to annihilate them. They would not surrender.'
>
> US General Collins, describing an attack on Guadalcanal: Television interview, 1973

The Second World War

Source B

'Between April and August 1945 21st Bomber Command ... destroyed 40 per cent of the built up area of 66 cities ... A combination of sea blockade and bombing reduced most Japanese industries to a mere fraction of their wartime peak. By July aluminium production was reduced to 9 per cent, oil refining and steel production to 15 per cent.'

Richard Overy: *Why the Allies Won* (1995)

Source C

'We said that we didn't think that being scientists especially qualified us as to how to answer this question of how the [A] bombs should be used or not ... We did say that we did not think that exploding one of these things as a firecracker over a desert was likely to be very impressive.'

Scientific panel advising US government in 1945

Source D

'The final decision of where and when to use the atomic bomb was up to me. Let there be no mistake about it. I regarded the bomb as a military weapon and never had any doubts that it should be used.'

US President Harry S Truman: *Memoirs* (1955)

Source E

'The decision to use the atomic bomb ... brought death to over a hundred thousand Japanese ... but this deliberate, premeditated destruction of Hiroshima and Nagasaki put an end to the Japanese war. It stopped the fire raids and the strangling blockade; it ended the ghastly spectre of a clash of great armies.'

Henry Stimson, US Secretary of War in 1945

Specimen question

1 Read Source D.
   (a) In what ways do you think the A bomb differed from other military weapons?
      [2 marks]
   (b) Why, do you think, did Harry Truman describe his decision to drop the bomb in such a matter-of-fact way? [3 marks]

Hints

Was the decision to drop the bomb controversial? Would Truman like controversy? How might he stop people criticising him?

Specimen questions

2 Read Sources A and C.
   How do these sources support dropping the bomb? [4 marks]

3 Read Source B.
   Do the facts quoted in this source argue against dropping the bomb? Explain your answer. [6 marks]

Hint

Remember there may be no right answer to this. Whatever you think, you must give good reasons for your view. That is what the examiner is interested in.

Model answer

Overy (Source B) shows that conventional bombing and the blockade were destroying Japanese towns and had badly damaged the country's industry. This meant that even without the A bomb Japan would probably have lost the war. But this doesn't disprove the case that the A bombs saved lives by ending the war quickly. This was the main argument in favour of using the bomb. So the source doesn't necessarily argue against dropping the bomb. In any case, President Truman could not have known at the time how weak Japanese industry was.

Specimen question

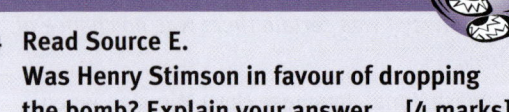

4 Read Source E.
   Was Henry Stimson in favour of dropping the bomb? Explain your answer. [4 marks]

Check

That you understand how and why Japan was defeated.

The bombing war

People still argue about the bombing war. Some say it was a waste of men, material and money. Others say it helped to shorten the war in Europe. You need to know how effective you think it was and to be able to back up your opinion with evidence.

British raids on Germany 1940–42

After the defeat of France, British bombers attacked German factories and railways. It was the only way Britain could attack Germany.

Source A

Heavy "Stirling" bombers raid the Nazi Baltic port of Lübeck and leave the docks ablaze

BACK THEM UP!

This poster shows British bombers attacking Lübeck

Source B

In 1941, after examining aerial photographs, a civil servant, D M Butt, worked out that only one in five of British bombers managed to get within nine miles of their target. In 1941, 1034 British bombers were shot down.

Specimen question

1 Would British civilians who had seen Source A have been surprised by the information in Source B? Explain your answer.　　　　　[4 marks]

Hint

Would they believe the poster?

Specimen question

2 Does Source B give the impression that the raids on Germany between 1940 and 1942 were effective?　[2 marks]

German raids on Britain 1940–42

Between 25 August and 4 September 1940 the British bombed Berlin five times. In revenge Hitler ordered the Luftwaffe to bomb British cities. Between September 1940 and March 1941 there were regular raids on British cities, killing 21,000 people. (*See* also Chapter 10.)

Source A

'*We shall obliterate their cities.*'
Hitler: Speech, 4 September 1940

Source B

'*Last Thursday 180 persons were killed in London as a result of 251 tons of bombs. That is to say it took one ton of bombs to kill three-quarters of a person ... It would take ten years, at the present rate of bombing, for half the houses of London to be demolished. [But] quite a lot of things are going to happen to Herr Hitler and the Nazi regime before ten years are up.*'
Winston Churchill: House of Commons speech, 8 October 1940

Source C

'You must try to picture the bombed-out as I saw them. White-faced, their homes and lives shattered . . . They had crept out of the shelter . . . They came past houses with no windows and no roofs, houses split and frontless . . . maybe with the furniture showing on each floor . . . And as a background to it all, the sirens wailing every few hours, and the drone of bombers overhead, and the whine and crash of bombs, and the everlasting sour smell of smoke.'

Frank R Lewey, Mayor of Stepney: Interview

Specimen questions

1   Was Hitler's threat to 'obliterate' Britain's cities realistic? Explain your answer. [4 marks]

2   Is Churchill's calculation in Source B to be trusted? Explain your answer. [4 marks]

Hints

How did Churchill know the exact tonnage of bombs dropped on London on a particular night? What were the aims of his speech in the House of Commons? How might they have biased what he said?

Specimen question

3   Source C describes what it was like to be bombed out of one's home. Yet Hitler's Blitz did not destroy civilian morale in Britain. Why was this? [6 marks]

Bombing Germany 1942–44

In 1942 Churchill met Stalin and promised to help the Soviet Union by bombing Germany. By this time 'Bomber' Harris was in charge of Bomber Command. He believed that bombing large towns would eventually destroy the morale of the people living there and disrupt their working lives, thus cutting production and hindering the war effort.

Facts and figures

Night raids
In March 1944, 1719 bombers were sent to Berlin. Only 27 dropped their bombs within 3 miles of the target.

Up to 10 per cent of the bombers were lost on every raid.

Daylight raids
In summer 1943, the US air force began daylight raids. These were more accurate.

More than 20 per cent of the bombers were lost on every raid.

German war production (000s)

	Planes	Tanks
1941	12	5
1942	15	9
1943	25	17
1944	40	22

Specimen question

Do the facts and figures prove that the Allied bombing of Germany at that time was ineffective? Explain your answer. [5 marks]

Hint

Statistics are tricky. Who is likely to have compiled the figures of German war production? Might they have falsified the figures? What about other commodities? And might the production of tanks and planes have been even higher without the bombing?

Bombing Germany 1944–45

By the end of 1943 the Allies had more heavy bombers and a new long-range fighter – the Mustang. For the first time fighters could escort bombers all the way to Germany and back. They also had more accurate equipment to guide them to their targets. As a result the war in the air over Germany changed.

Source A

'The standard of the Americans is extraordinarily high. Our day fighters have lost more than 1,000 aircraft during the last few months, including our best officers. The gaps cannot be filled.'

Adolf Galland, German Luftwaffe General: *The First and the Last* (1955)

Source B

'There are about 1,000 heavy bombers flying eastwards … with a strong fighter escort … Against them we are forty aircraft.'

H Knoke, a German fighter pilot: 1944 diary

Source C

Tons of bombs dropped on Germany	
1939–44	240,000
1944–45	1,180,000

Source D

'One can't get used to the raids. I wished for an end. We all got nerves. We did not get enough sleep and were very tense. People fainted when they heard the first bomb drop.'

Worker at a Munich factory, 1945

Source E

'The war is over in the area of heavy industry and armament.'

Albert Speer, Minister in charge of War Production: Report to Hitler, January 1945

Source F

'American air intelligence exaggerated German air strength in 1940 by a factor of ten … A new generation of bombers, fighters and fighter bombers … were produced in greater numbers than were needed … to match what it was believed Germany was producing.'

Richard Overy: *Why the Allies Won* (1995)

Specimen questions

1 **What evidence is there that by 1945 Bomber Harris had been proved right?**
   [4 marks]

2 **What developments made it possible for Allied bombers to destroy German industry by 1945?**
   [4 marks]

3 **What evidence is there that the Allied success in the air war was based on a mistake? Explain your answer.**
   [4 marks]

Check

That you can explain how the bombing war changed between 1939 and 1945 and how important it was.

The Home Front

The Second World War affected life in Britain in many ways. In some ways – shortages, conscription, rationing – the effects were much the same as in the First World War. But other effects, like bombing, invasion and propaganda, were different. *See* also pages 123–28.

Bombing

The government expected Britain to be bombed and gassed in the Second World War. So they had prepared for it by building shelters, distributing gas masks, enforcing a blackout, evacuating children from London and other large cities and enlisting voluntary 'wardens' to organise air raid precautions such as watching out for fires caused by incendiary bombs.

Source

A poster asking for women to join the fire service

Specimen questions

1   What job, usually performed by firemen, is not mentioned in the list of duties to be performed by women members of the fire service? Why was this, do you think?   [3 marks]

2   Compare this poster with the WRAF recruiting poster in Chapter 1. Is there any evidence that the official attitude to what women could do had changed since 1917? Explain your answer.   [4 marks]

Invasion

In the First World War Britain was never likely to be invaded. In 1940 it seemed very likely, so the government took precautions, building defences, taking down road signs, and setting up the volunteer Home Guard.

Warning!

Dad's Army is a comedy programme not a documentary.

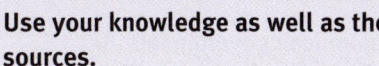

Propaganda

Propaganda was very important. The coming of radio made it possible to broadcast messages very widely, very quickly. Churchill used it a lot, but both sides broadcast propaganda to their enemies. Both sides also used films, posters and newspapers to get their message across.

Source A

'We shall go on to the end. We shall fight in France, we shall fight on the seas and oceans, we shall fight with growing confidence and growing strength in the air, we shall defend our island, whatever the cost may be. We shall fight on the beaches, we shall fight on the landing grounds, we shall fight in the fields and in the streets, we shall fight in the hills; we shall never surrender.'

Winston Churchill: House of Commons speech, 4 June 1940

Source B

'That was worth 1,000 guns, and the speeches of 1,000 years.'

Josiah Wedgwood, Labour MP, after hearing Churchill's speech

Source C

'The Nation had the lion's heart. I had the luck to give the roar.'

Winston Churchill: Speech, 1954

Specimen questions

1   What effect did Churchill hope his 1940 speech would have on
    (a) the British people
    (b) the Germans?   [4 marks]

2   What evidence is there that the speech was successful?   [3 marks]

Hint

Use your knowledge as well as the sources.

Specimen question

3   Do you think that Churchill's estimate of his importance in the war was correct? Explain your answer.   [10 marks]

Hint

Did he help to give the nation its heart as well as supply the roar? What about his actions and policies?

Check

That you understand the effects that the war had on Britain.

The Weimar Republic

Foundation

In November 1918 there was a revolution in Germany. The Kaiser's government, dominated by the army, was swept away and replaced at a conference which met at Weimar by a democratically elected government. Most of the new ministers were lawyers and businessmen. The President, Friedrich Ebert, for instance, had worked as a saddler and journalist. The *Reichstag* (Parliament) was elected by proportional representation. As a result it contained a number of small parties, so that no one party ever had a majority of seats. So governments tended to be weak and divided. Almost their first job was to sign the Treaty of Versailles (*see* Chapter 2).

Source A

'I make no bones of the fact that I am a monarchist. My God! when a man has served his king and country faithfully for 30 years he can't suddenly say, "Starting tomorrow I'm a republican." '

Colonel William Reinhard, quoted in O Schuddekopf: *Das Heer und die Republik* (1955)

Source B

'A dazzling lieutenant is of greater importance than the mayor of a great city. The latter may walk through the streets unrecognised, but every policeman, tram-conductor, post or railway official salutes an officer.'

Richard Hanser: *Prelude to Terror* (1971)

Source C

'May the hand wither that signs this treaty'

Philip Scheidemann, German Chancellor: Speech, June 1919

Specimen questions

Study the sources.

1 How far do Sources A and B help to explain why many Germans never had any respect for the Weimar government?   [4 marks]

2 Check on the terms of the Treaty of Versailles (*see* Chapter 2). Explain why Chancellor Scheidemann was so opposed to signing it.   [10 marks]

1923 – a critical year

1923 was an important year for the Weimar Republic. The French and Belgians occupied the Ruhr; the mark lost all its value (*see* Chapter 2). Finally, in the Munich *Putsch*, Adolf Hitler tried to take over the government.

In September 1923 the Bavarian state government declared a state of emergency. Some thought they intended to make Bavaria independent of the rest of Germany. The timeline will remind you of what happened next.

Munich Putsch timeline

8 November 1923	Adolf Hitler took over a political meeting in Munich and captured Bavarian government leaders.
9 November 1923	Hitler's march through Munich was dispersed by armed police.
February 1924	Hitler found guilty of treason. Sentenced to five years' imprisonment.
December 1924	Hitler released from prison, having written part one of *Mein Kampf*.

The prosperous years 1925–29

Between 1925 and 1929 Germany prospered on money borrowed from the USA. The country became famous for its artists and architects. Berlin also became famous for its night life.

Source

A cartoon entitled 'Lovers' little hour' by George Grasz, a left-wing cartoonist. The cartoon shows a rich businessman entertaining a prostitute

The Crash

In 1929, after the Wall Street Crash, Americans wanted Germany to repay the money she had borrowed. Suddenly there was no money to spare in Germany. People bought fewer goods. Factories closed and unemployment rose.

German unemployment	
1928	650,000
1929	1,320,000
1930	3,000,000
1931	4,350,000
1932	6,000,000

Specimen question

Why, by 1932, did many Germans want to be rid of the Weimar government?

[15 marks]

Hint

The Weimar government was unpopular for several reasons:

* it had consented to the Treaty of Versailles
* the economy was weakened by unemployment and inflation
* too many political parties made government unstable
* strikes, conflict and political violence increased
* the ministers and President were considered weak and unimpressive
* some felt social behaviour and morals were declining

Check

That you understand why the Weimar government was weak and unpopular.

The rise of Hitler

Hitler and the Nazi Party were ready to sweep away the whole Weimar system.

A reminder of the Nazi Party belief system and their methods:

* loyalty to Germany essential
* racial purity: Aryans (white Europeans) were the master race and other races, especially Jews, were inferior
* equality and state control of the economy
* the German people needed to expand into other territories
* the Führer (leader) commanded total loyalty
* control of the people via propaganda, rallies, speeches, etc. and through the use of strong policing, e.g. the SS

The high point of many party meetings and rallies was a speech by Hitler himself.

Source A

'One must be able to say once again: German people, hold your heads high and proudly once more! You are no longer enslaved and in bondage, but you are free again and can truly say: "We are all proud that through God's powerful aid we have once more become true Germans."'

Hitler: Extract from a speech made in March 1933

Source B

'I was held under a hypnotic spell by the sheer force of his conviction. The intense will of the man, the passion of his sincerity, seemed to flow from him into me. It was like a religious conversion.'

A listener to one of Hitler's speeches in 1922

Hitler's rise timeline

1920–23	Hitler organised the Nazi Party.
1923	German inflation. The Munich Putsch.
1924	Hitler imprisoned – wrote *Mein Kampf*.
1925–29	Germany prosperous – Nazis won little support.
1929	Wall Street Crash.
1930	German unemployment reached 15 per cent. Nazis won 107 Reichstag seats.
1932	Unemployment 30 per cent. Nazis won 230 seats (July); 197 seats (November).
1933	Hitler became Chancellor (Prime Minister).

Tip

Notice how much information can be crammed into a mini timeline. Compile your own to help with your revision.

Specimen question

'The main reason for Hitler's growing support was the unpopularity of the Weimar governments.' Do you agree? Explain your answer fully.   [15 marks]

Hints

As usual in questions such as this you need to show that other factors too were at work. If the unpopularity of the government was the most important factor, why didn't people vote Communist? They opposed Weimar too. So there must have been positive reasons. Hitler's patriotism? Hitler's confidence – compare with Roosevelt? Hitler's skill as an orator, his use of the media, the slick organisation of his meetings, etc.

The 1932 elections

The 1932 elections were very violent.

Source A

'There were between 1st June and 20th July in Prussia . . . 322 serious clashes involving 72 deaths and 497 injured. Prominent socialists and communists were surprised at night and murdered in their beds or shot down at the doors of their houses. The windows of shops owned by Jews were smashed and their contents looted whilst attacks with high explosives were directed against the offices of democratically-owned newspapers.'

Sir Horace Rumbold, British Ambassador in Berlin: Dispatch to the British Foreign Office, 1932

Source B

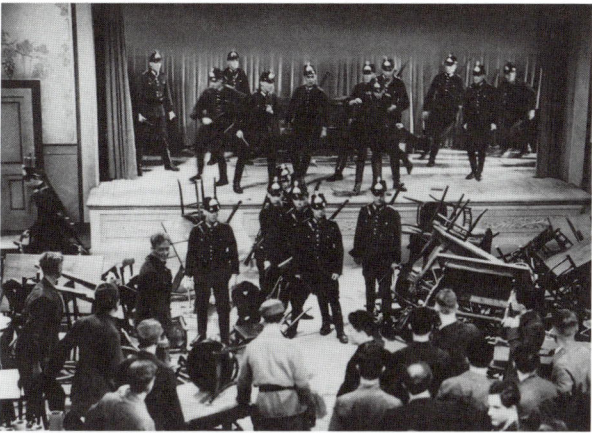

Police in a public hall following an election meeting

Specimen question

1   Study Sources A and B. Which of the two is more convincing evidence that the 1932 elections were violent? Explain your answer.   [5 marks]

Hints

Who wrote Source A? Were the figures he quoted likely to be reliable? Remember it was an important official document, written to tell his government what was going on in Germany. What does Source B prove? Might, for instance, the police have moved in to prevent disorder and cleared the hall? How much does a photograph of one incident tell you about the situation in the country as a whole?

Specimen question

2   What evidence is there in Source A that Hitler's supporters were responsible for much of the violence he described?
                    [5 marks]

Check

That you understand how Hitler came to be Chancellor.

Hitler becomes Führer

The Reichstag fire

Once he had become Chancellor, Hitler decided to hold a fresh election in March 1933 to try to win more seats. On 27 February the Reichstag building in Berlin was burnt to the ground. A young Dutch Communist, Marianus van der Lubbe, was arrested on the spot and later executed for the crime.

After the fire Hitler claimed that it proved that the Communists were planning to take over the state. He proclaimed a state of emergency giving himself wide powers. He imprisoned anti-Nazis and censored anti-Nazi newspapers. In the election the Nazis won 330 out of 647 seats.

Source

THE REICHSTAG IN FLAMES

Set alight by the Communists! This is what the whole country would look like if Communism and its ally Social Democracy were to come to power only for a few months!

Innocent citizens shot as hostages!

Farmers' houses burnt down!

All Germany must join the outcry:

Stamp Out Communism!

Smash Social Democracy!

VOTE FOR HITLER

Nazi election leaflet, 1933

Specimen questions

1 In what ways was the leaflet misleading? **[5 marks]**

2 What impression does it give of Hitler's aims? **[4 marks]**

3 Why was it that many of Hitler's opponents claimed that the Nazis themselves burned down the Reichstag building? **[6 marks]**

On 23 March the Reichstag passed an Enabling Act, by 441 votes to 94, giving Hitler absolute power.

The Night of the Long Knives 1934

Hitler's uniformed storm troopers – the SA (*Sturmabteilung*) – had helped him in his campaign to become Chancellor by policing his meetings, beating up his opponents, collecting money and organising marches and demonstrations. By 1934 there were 3 million of them. Their commander was Ernst Röhm.

German army officers hated the SA. In 1934 President Hindenburg was dying, and Hitler wanted to take over from him. To do this he needed the support of the army. On 30 June (The Night of the Long Knives), on Hitler's orders, about 900 prominent SA members, including

Röhm, were arrested and shot. In August Hindenburg died and Hitler took over, declaring himself 'Führer' (Leader) of Germany. From then on he relied on the SS (*Schutzstaffel*) under Heinrich Himmler to enforce his wishes.

Source A

'Revolution is not a permanent condition . . . The ideas in our programme impose an obligation on us not to act like fools and to overthrow everything.'

Hitler: Speech, July 1933

Source B

'Are we revolutionaries or aren't we? . . . If we're not, then we'll go to the dogs.'

Ernst Röhm: Interview, 1934

Source C

'The government isn't going to last long. The main thing for me is that I've got work through the SA. I played along till then. Now the SA can go to blazes.'

Gestapo report on an SA member in Essen

Source D

'I swear to thee, Adolf Hitler . . . Loyalty and Bravery. I vow to thee and to the superiors whom thou shalt appoint obedience unto death, so help me God.'

Oath sworn by SS members

Specimen question

1 Read the sources. In what ways do they add to the account of the reasons for the Night of the Long Knives given in the text? **[10 marks]**

Hints

Policy clashes between Röhm and Hitler? Trustworthiness of SA compared with SS? Remember to refer to the sources in your answer.

The rise of Himmler and the SS timeline

1925 *Schutzstaffel* (SS) set up within the SA to guard Nazi leaders.

1929 SS numbered about 200. Himmler put in charge.

1933 Himmler put in charge of secret police over most of Germany. Set up first concentration camp at Dachau. The SS later administered all the 'death camps'.

1934 SS had 50,000 members. Made independent of the SA. Himmler put in charge of Gestapo (Prussian secret police).

1936 All German criminal police merged with secret police under Himmler.

1939 Himmler appointed 'Commissioner for strengthening German Folkdom', that is, eliminating the Jews.

1940 *Waffen* (armed) SS set up to fight under Himmler's control. Eventually numbered 600,000 men.

1943 Himmler and SS put in charge of the German rocket programme.

Specimen question

2   What evidence is there in the timeline that Hitler had a continuing trust in Himmler?   **[4 marks]**

Check

That you understand how Hitler became Führer.

The German economy 1933–39

Hitler believed that the Germans were the master race. So he was determined to create a strong, stable, independent and beautiful country for them to live in and to make sure that they all had work with enough pay for them to live pleasant and prosperous lives. The spider diagram below will remind you of Hitler's economic policies.

Notes

*   The LSO was the Labour Service Organisation which provided work for school leavers building sea walls, draining marshes and other such jobs.
*   Autarky means that a country produces everything that it needs, not having to rely on imports. Hitler wanted Germany to achieve this. He did not succeed.

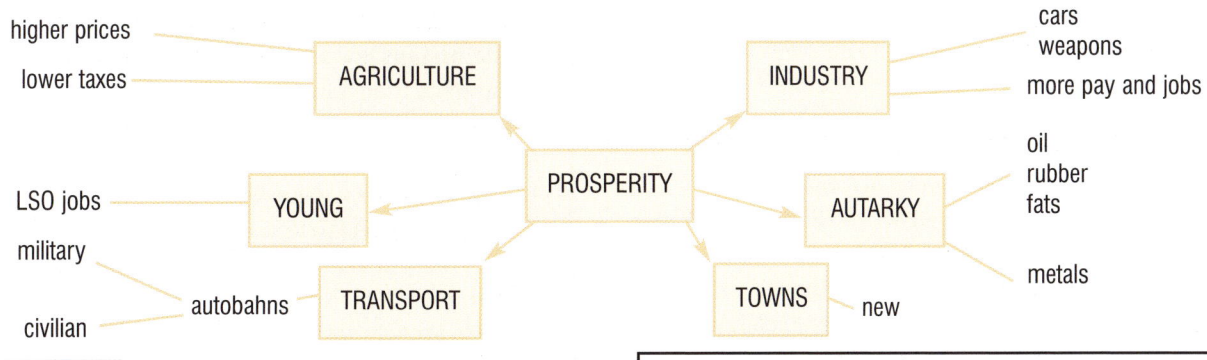

Source A

Unemployment (millions)

1932	5.6	1936	1.6
1933	4.8	1937	0.9
1934	2.7	1938	0.4
1935	2.2		

Production percentages

	1928	1932	1935	1938
Coal	100	69	95	123
Steel	100	33	109	154
Chemicals	100	51	79	127
Household goods	100	70	80	114

Source B

A 'Strength Through Joy' poster advertising cheap travel for German workers. The caption reads 'Now you too can travel'

Source C

'He [Hitler] is a great and wonderful leader. He is the saviour of Germany.'

David Lloyd George: Interview, 1936

Source D

'[In 1951] almost half of those citizens of the Federal Republic of Germany questioned in a public opinion survey described the period between 1933 and 1939 as one in which things had gone best for Germany.'

Ulrich Herbert: *Life in the Third Reich* (1987)

Specimen question

'The information in Sources A, B and C is enough to account for the happy memories of Germany in the 1930s mentioned in Source D.' Do you agree? Explain your answer fully.

[12 marks]

Hints

To get good marks you need to analyse what the sources show and use your own knowledge to indicate what they leave out.

Model answer

The sources show that after 1933 the German economy steadily improved. Source A shows that industrial production grew, until by 1938 it was more than in 1928 in all sectors. At the same time unemployment was falling steadily to less than half a million in 1938. Source B shows that the government made sure that workers benefited, laying on opportunities for travel never before available to ordinary working people. Source C shows that in Hitler they had a leader who was admired by visiting statesmen. All these things might be remembered with pleasure.

But other changes, not mentioned in the sources, also appealed to the German people. The sources do not mention agriculture. Hitler made sure that the incomes of farmers increased. Law and order is also left out. For most Germans law and order was much better maintained than it had been under Weimar. Finally, the sources do not say anything about foreign policy. Hitler's decisions to leave the League of Nations, to begin to rearm, to enter the Rhineland and to unite with Austria in spite of the Treaty of Versailles were all very popular. So although the information in the sources helps to account for the happy memories, the sources don't tell the whole story.

Check

That you understand how the German economy improved under Hitler.

Life under the Nazis

Keeping control

The spider diagram below will remind you of the methods used by Hitler to keep control of Germany.

The law

Hitler controlled the law. He could make new laws by decree, and if he did not like the way a court was working he abolished it and replaced it by another.

Source A

'The Law and the Führer are one.'

H Göring to a meeting of Prussian lawyers in 1934

Source B

'Say to yourselves at every decision which you make: "How would the Führer decide in my place?"'

Dr Hans Frank, Commissioner of Justice, to a conference of judges in 1936

Source C

'As the prisoner refused to give information he was tortured ... He was held by three assistants while the official and another assistant took turns in beating him with a flexible leather-covered steel rod. When he fainted from pain and loss of blood he was brought to by means of various other tortures.'

Account of a Gestapo officer in Hamburg: *Manchester Guardian*, 1 July 1935

Specimen questions

1 How did the Nazi system of justice ensure that Hitler's wishes were carried out? [6 marks]

2 What evidence is there that the Nazis believed their system of law was one to be proud of? [5 marks]

Hint

Is there any evidence in the sources that they tried to conceal the system? Or did they boast about it?

Check

That you understand how the Nazis administered the law.

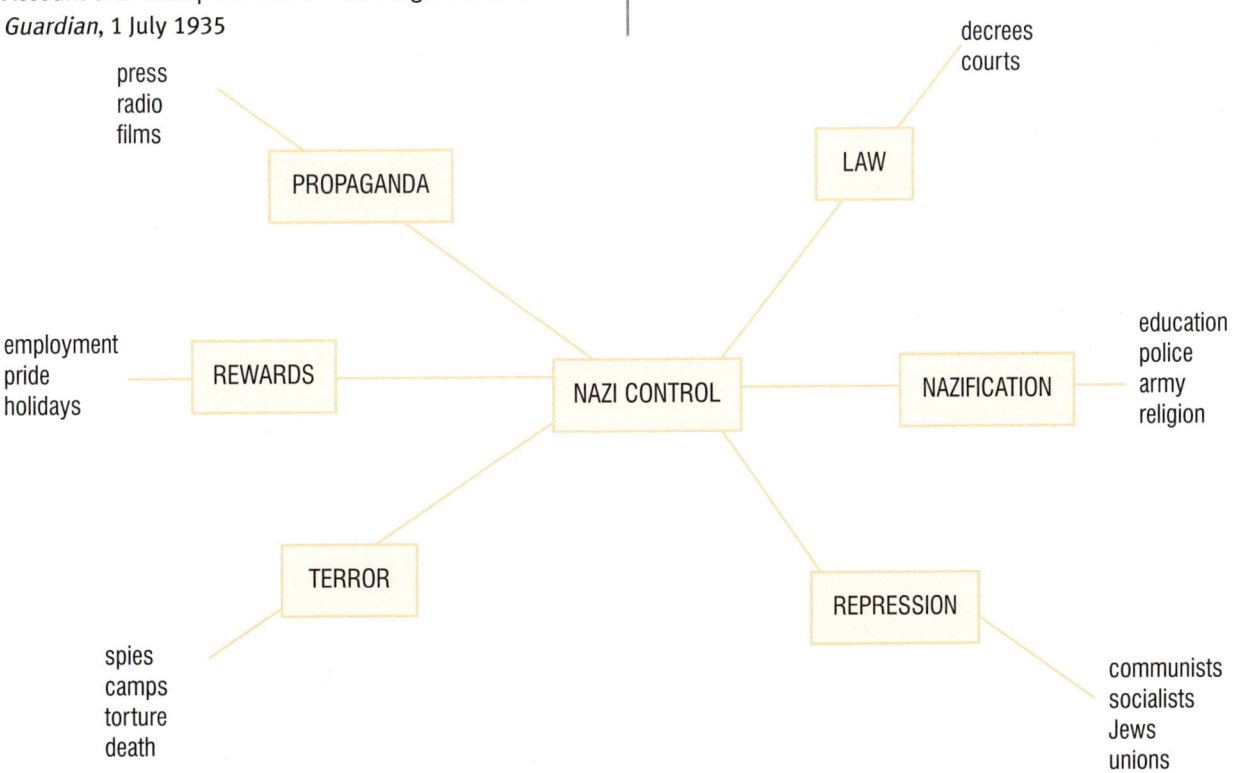

PROPAGANDA — press, radio, films

LAW — decrees, courts

REWARDS — employment, pride, holidays

NAZI CONTROL

NAZIFICATION — education, police, army, religion

TERROR — spies, camps, torture, death

REPRESSION — communists, socialists, Jews, unions

Hitler Youth

Hitler Youth timeline

1933	Rival youth groups except church groups banned.
1935	Civil servants ordered to send their children to Hitler Youth.
1936	Church youth groups banned.
1939	All young people ordered to join Hitler Youth.

Source A

'All of the German youth in the Reich is organised within the Hitler Youth ... The German Youth shall be educated physically, intellectually and morally in the spirit of National Socialism ... through the Hitler Youth.'

Adolf Hitler: Decree, December 1936

Source C

'In the presence of this blood banner which represents our Führer, I swear to devote all my energies and my strength to the saviour of our country, Adolf Hitler. I am willing and ready to give up my life for him, so help me God.'

Oath taken by Hitler Youth boys

Source D

'No one in our class ever read Mein Kampf. I myself only took quotations from the book. On the whole we didn't know very much about ideology ... Nevertheless we were politically programmed: to obey orders, to cultivate the soldierly "virtue" of standing to attention and saying "Yes, Sir" and to stop thinking when the magic word "Fatherland" was uttered.'

An anonymous German quoted in Detler Peukert: *Youth in the Third Reich* (1987)

Source E

'I was sent for my period of Community Service to a camp in East Prussia. This time was the most carefree of my life. During the harvesting we used to work more than fifteen hours a day. We were so tired I could hardly stand up. But I was so happy because I felt useful. Among us there were country girls, students, hairdressers, domestic servants.'

Melita Maschmann in *The Encyclopaedia of the Second World War*

Source B

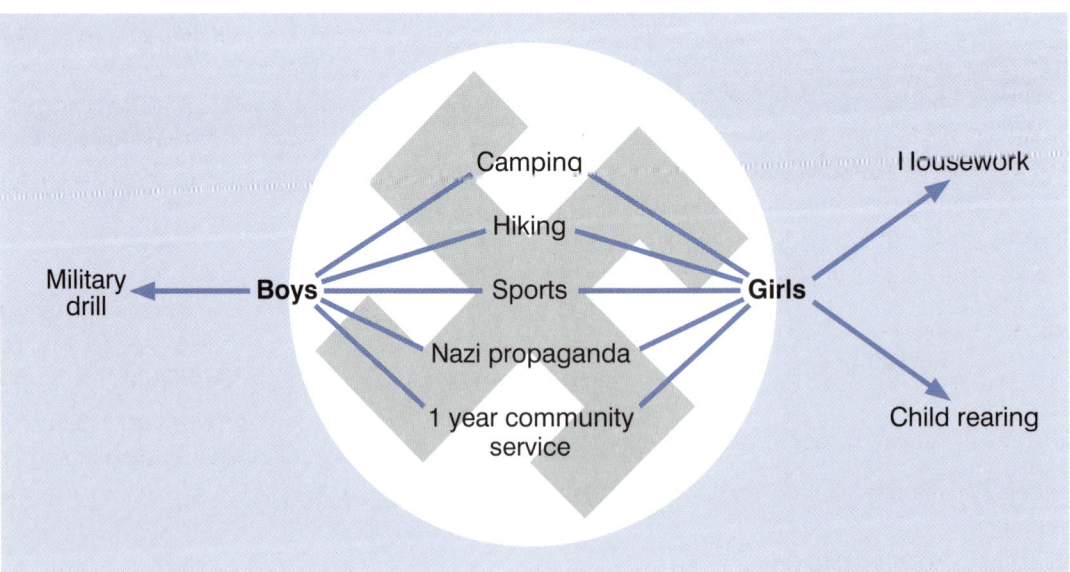

Hitler Youth activities

Specimen questions

1 What evidence is there that Nazis believed that the Hitler Youth movement would strengthen Hitler's hold on Germany? [5 marks]

2 To what extent does Source D cast doubt on the effectiveness of the Hitler Youth programme? [6 marks]

Hints

How typical might the young German's reaction have been? Did the fact that he did not know much about ideology matter so long as he did what he was told?

Specimen questions

3 Girls' activities in Hitler Youth differed in some ways from those of boys. Explain the difference. [4 marks]

4 To what extent does Source E show that Hitler Youth was a force for good? [10 marks]

Hints

Ten marks demands an extended answer, perhaps along these lines: 'The extract might show that some aspects of Hitler Youth were good' – give examples 'but other aspects were not' – give examples. Then balance the two.

Schools

Hitler reformed the German school system:

- All teachers had to promise to be 'loyal and obedient to Adolf Hitler'.
- The number of girls allowed into higher education was drastically cut.
- In History, pupils learned that Germans were the master race, and that the Jews caused all the evil in the world.
- In Biology they learned that it was vital to keep the German race pure.
- In Physics and Chemistry they ignored discoveries made by Jewish scientists.
- Pupils were encouraged to study *Mein Kampf*.
- Hitler set up special schools, concentrating on competitive sports, to educate future leaders.

Specimen question

What effect would you expect Hitler's school reforms to have on scientific knowledge and research in Germany? Explain your answer. [4 marks]

Check

That you understand how the Hitler Youth movement worked.

Hitler's opponents

When Hitler came to power in 1933 he was opposed by democratic political parties and by the Communists, amongst others (*see* Source C on page 82).

Source A

'The sole political party existing in Germany is the National Socialist German Workers' Party . . . Whoever shall undertake to maintain the organisation of another party, or to start a new party, shall be punished with a sentence of hard labour of up to three years.'

Law Against the New Formation of Parties, 14 July 1933

Source B

(A lawyer's client was tried and found not guilty under the 14 July law.)

'He was just in time to see his client being marched away between two uniformed guards and bundled into a green van . . . [His] client had vanished without trace.'

C Bielenberg (the lawyer's wife): *The Past is Myself* (1984)

This table lists some of Hitler's opponents in Germany, shows why they opposed him and what happened to them. The list is not complete.

Socialists and Communists	Opposed most of Hitler's policies.	Camps, prisons, executions
Trade Unionists	Wanted to organise workers independently of the Nazis.	Camps, prisons, executions
Ernst Röhm	Leader of the SA. Wanted a more revolutionary policy (1934).	Killed (Night of Long Knives)
Martin Niemöller	Protestant pastor. Opposed Nazification of Church.	Concentration camp 1937–45
'July' Generals	Tried to assassinate Hitler to end war in 1944.	About 4900 executed or killed themselves
Dietrich Bonhoeffer	Lutheran pastor. Joined July conspiracy.	Executed 1945

Source D

[At the end of 1944] 'the fact seems beyond dispute – the great proportion of the German people still believed in Adolf Hitler.'

General Heinz Guderian: *Panzer Leader* (1952)

Specimen question

1 Why was there no organised political opposition to Hitler after 1933?

[5 marks]

Hint

Remember to refer to Source A *and* Source B in your answer.

Specimen question

2 Do you think the lawyer (Source B) was running a risk in defending his client? Explain your answer.   [4 marks]

Hint

Consider his status as a lawyer on the one hand, as against the ruthlessness of the Nazis on the other.

Specimen question

3 Does the fate of Hitler's opponents outlined in Source C account for the German people's professed support for Hitler as reported in Source D? Explain your answer fully.   [15 marks]

Hints

As always, suspect the offer of one, simple explanation. In this case you could point out that the statement in Source D that they 'believed in' Hitler contradicts the view that they only supported him out of fear. Also, consider: gratitude for his past achievements (mention some); the effect of propaganda; patriotic support for the leader in wartime; the lack of any alternative leader.

Check

That you understand why the opposition to Hitler failed.

The impact of war

Rearmament

In 1936 Hitler ordered Göring to launch a four-year plan to rearm in preparation for a large-scale war beginning any time after 1940.

In 1942 Hitler put Albert Speer in charge of the German armaments industry. Production increased.

Source A

Financial statistics (billions of marks)		
	Spent on rearmament	Size of National Debt
1935	5.4	15.9
1936	10.2	20.1
1937	10.9	25.8
1938	17.2	31.2

Source B

'With the extension of the period of compulsory military service to two years on 24 August 1936, the constitution of military works . . . and, beginning in 1938–39 the addition of naval re-armament to the army and air force programmes, the situation became so acute as to necessitate the direction of labour.'

K Hildebrand: *The Third Reich* (1984)

Source C

'The construction of the navy as ordered by me, must have priority over all other tasks in armaments including those of the other two branches of the armed forces.'

Adolf Hitler: Directive in January 1939

Source D

'When the German army attacked Russia in 1941 only a third of the force was fully equipped with German arms. Most of the rest had some equipment captured from France and Czechoslovakia or else were short of some of their weapons.'

John Patrick: *Hindsight* (1995)

Specimen questions

1   Study Source A. How did the Nazi government pay for increased rearmament before 1939?   [2 marks]

2   What evidence is there in Sources B, C and D that the arms drive was poorly organised?   [4 marks]

3   Had Göring fulfilled Hitler's order to prepare for a large-scale war by 1940? Explain your answer.   [5 marks]

Life in wartime

The spider diagram below will show you the effects of the war on life in Germany. Remember that conditions gradually got worse as the war went on.

Goods and people from conquered countries were brought back to Germany during the war.

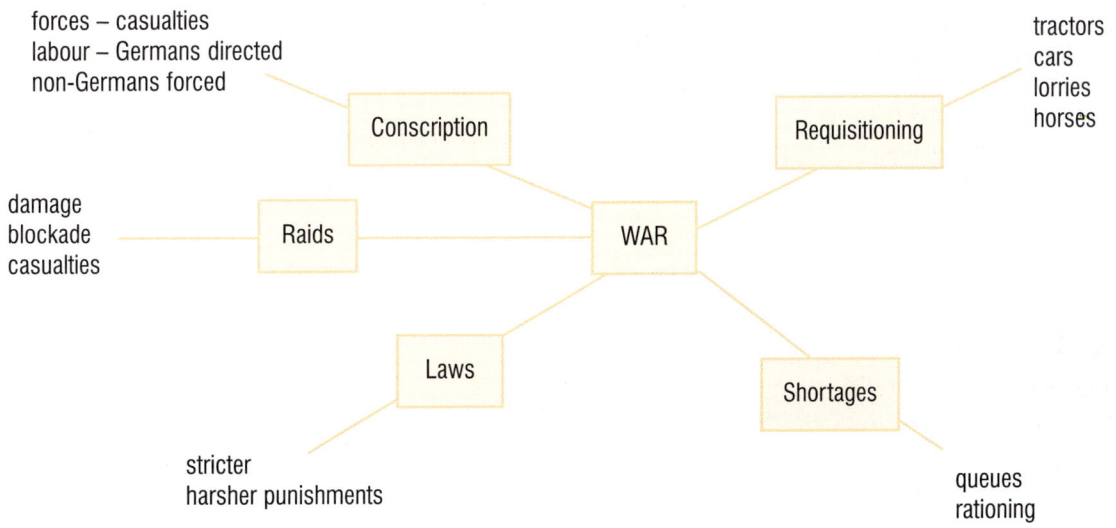

forces – casualties
labour – Germans directed
non-Germans forced

tractors
cars
lorries
horses

damage
blockade
casualties

Conscription

Requisitioning

Raids

WAR

Laws

Shortages

stricter
harsher punishments

queues
rationing

Source A

'Whenever you come across anything that may be needed by the German people you must be after it like a bloodhound. It must be . . . brought to Germany.'

H Göring: Instruction quoted in the Nuremberg war crime trials

Source B

'The Slavs are here to work for us. In so far as we don't need them, they may die.'

Martin Bormann, Hitler's deputy: Letter, 1942

Source C

'They . . . went about in their bare feet. The sole clothing of each consisted of a sack with holes for their arms and head . . . The amount of food in their camp was extremely meagre and of very poor quality. One could not enter their barracks without being attacked by fleas.'

Dr Wilhelm Jaeger: Evidence at the Nuremberg trials on foreign workers at a wartime Krupps munitions factory

Specimen questions

1 What does Source A tell us about the Nazi leaders' attitude to the people of the occupied countries? **[3 marks]**

2 What do Sources B and C tell us about their attitude to those working in forced labour camps? **[4 marks]**

3 How might the Nazis have justified their point of view? **[4 marks]**

Hint

Think about Nazi racial theories.

Check

That you understand how life in Germany changed in wartime.

Hitler and the Jews

All his life Hitler hated Jews. Once he was in power he began to harass them (*see* the timeline).

Jewish persecution timeline

1933		Government organised boycott of Jewish shops, lawyers and doctors.
1935		All official positions barred to non-Germans. 'Mixed' marriages forbidden.
1937		Some Jewish businesses confiscated.
1938	**April**	Jewish wealth registered.
	June	Jewish businesses registered.
	Oct	17,000 Jews expelled from Germany.
	Nov	'Crystal Night': 7500 Jewish shops destroyed, 400 synagogues burnt down. 20,000 Jews imprisoned. Jewish pupils excluded from schools.
	Dec	Jewish businesses and valuables confiscated.
1939		Jews ordered to live in special Jewish houses.
1940		Wholesale deportation of Jews began.
1942		Massed gassing of Jews began at Auschwitz.

It is generally agreed that by the end of the war the Nazis had killed about 6 million Jews, 2.5 million of whom came from Poland.

Source A

'Above all, I charge the leaders of the nation and those under them to . . . merciless opposition to the universal poisoner of all peoples, international Jewry.'

Hitler: *Political Testament* (April 1945)

Source B

'I saw the crematorium and realised for the first time that things like that do exist, because we have heard a lot of stories of those things but . . . you just can't realise it can be true and you thought, "Well, not really, people exaggerate" . . . But this was the first time that it hit home that it's true and the chances are that you will get killed.'

Concentration camp survivor: BBC documentary

Specimen questions

1 What evidence convinced the speaker in Source B that his life was in danger? **[2 marks]**

2 After the war many Germans claimed that they did not know that extermination camps existed. Does this seem likely? Refer to Source B and to your own knowledge. **[6 marks]**

3 Some historians claim that Hitler would not have approved of the extermination of the Jews. Does Source A disprove this view? **[6 marks]**

Hints

You need a lot of evidence to disprove a view. First, is the source likely to represent Hitler's real views? When was it written? Why? Is it consistent with what he wrote or said at other times? Next, does what he wrote amount to approval of the extermination of the Jews?

Check

That you understand how the Nazis tried to exterminate the Jews.

Preview

What you need to know:

- **How relations between the USSR and its wartime allies got worse after 1945**

- **How the Soviet government sited nuclear missiles in Cuba, and how the US government persuaded the USSR to remove them**

- **How the USA became involved in the war in Vietnam, and how they withdrew**

- **The growing unrest in the Eastern Bloc countries following the death of Stalin in 1953**

- **Why the United Nations was founded, how it was organised, how it has changed and how it acted in Korea and the Congo**

The beginning of the Cold War
The Iron Curtain

During the war, at conferences in Teheran (1943), Yalta (1945) and Potsdam (1945), the Allied leaders agreed that the Soviet Union should continue to control Eastern Europe after the war, and that Germany should be divided between the four Allies – Britain, France, the USA and the USSR.

The Soviet Union set up Communist governments in all the countries they controlled (*see* map).

> **Source A**

'You had the state planning system everywhere . . . You had communist parties . . . central committees, Politbureaux, Stalin pictures. You had the same party education materials.'

Wolfgang Leonhard, East German Communist Party official: BBC documentary, 1985

- Communist states dominated by USSR
- Communist but neutral
- European states in NATO
- The Iron Curtain

'An iron curtain has descended'

Source B

'From Stettin in the Baltic to Trieste in the Adriatic, an iron curtain has descended across the continent. Behind this line ... famous cities and the population around them lie in what I must call the Soviet sphere ... Communist fifth columns are established and work in complete unity and absolute obedience to the directions they receive from the Communist centre.'

Winston Churchill: Speech, Fulton, Missouri, 1946

Specimen questions

1 Why do you think Churchill called the frontier between the Soviet sphere and Western Europe 'an iron curtain'? [2 marks]

2 Which part of Churchill's speech does Source A seem to support? Explain your answer. [4 marks]

The Marshall Plan

President Truman of the USA feared that the USSR intended to take over the whole of Europe. So in 1947, by the Truman Doctrine, he promised that the USA would help any country threatened by the USSR and, by the Marshall Plan, the USA promised to pay $5000 million a year to help to strengthen friendly countries including, if they wished, the Soviet Union.

Source A

'Our policy is not directed against any country or doctrine, but against hunger, poverty, desperation and chaos. Its purpose should be the revival of ... political and social conditions in which free institutions can exist.'

General George Marshall: Speech, June 1947

Source B

'The American imperialists ... have taken the path of outright expansion, of enslaving the weakened capitalist states ... They have chosen the path of hatching new war plans against the Soviet Union and the new democracies ... The clearest expression of the policy is provided by the Truman–Marshall plans.'

Georgi Malenkov, Soviet Deputy Prime Minister: Speech, 1947

Specimen question

1 Do you believe Marshall when he says his plan was 'not directed against any country or doctrine'? Explain your answer. [3 marks]

Hint

Would Marshall have thought of a communist government as a 'free institution'?

Specimen question

2 What did Malenkov say was the real aim of the Marshall Plan? How could he have justified this view? [3 marks]

The Berlin blockade 1948

When Germany and the city of Berlin were divided into occupation zones at the end of the war, everyone took it for granted that a peace treaty would soon be signed and the occupation would end. But by 1948 the four former Allies were on such bad terms that there was no chance of a treaty. So the British and American governments began to unite their zones. In 1948 they tried to persuade the USSR to agree that the two zones could use the same currency. The Russians refused. The British and Americans went ahead anyway.

In June 1948 the USSR closed the road, rail and canal links between West Germany and Berlin. They had blockaded the city. The Allies supplied Berlin by air (*see map on page 88*). A cargo plane landed on average every two minutes. On 12 May, 1949, the Russians reopened the road, railway and canal links.

Source A

'War has left Russia with deep concern about German aggression. They are determined to stop the growth of a strong and possibly hostile Germany in the future.'

US Ambassador in Moscow: Dispatch, 1947

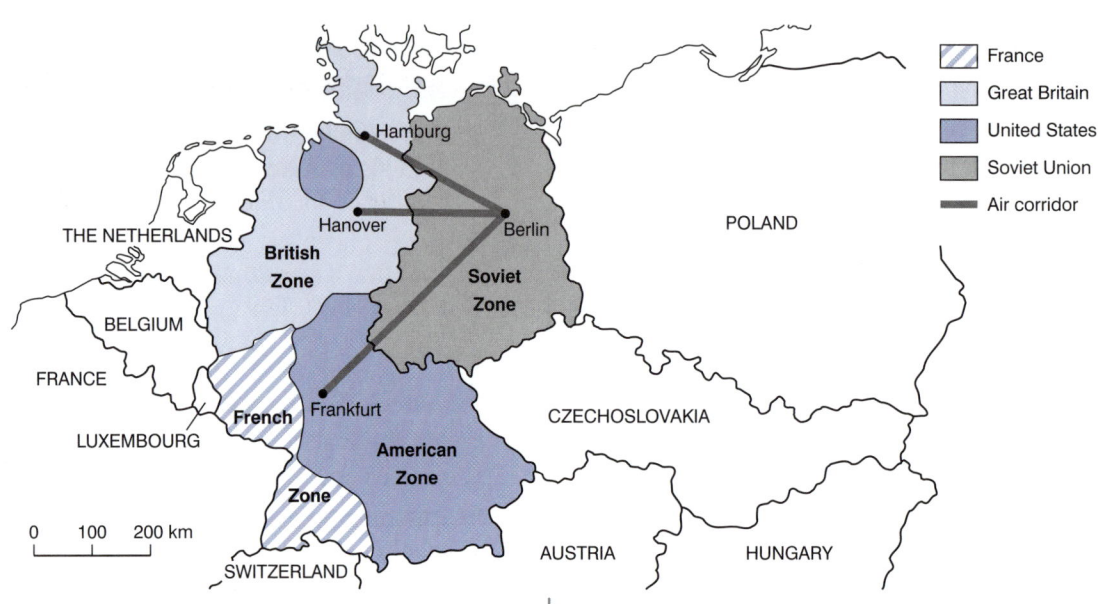

Occupied Germany from 1945

Source B

'There was no real choice. Either we did it, or West Berlin was lost to us. We were fairly sure that the Russians didn't want a showdown at that time – not sufficiently recovered from the war, but you can never be sure about that kind of thing, and we certainly weren't at that time.'

Clement Attlee, British Prime Minister, speaking in 1955

Source C

'We have lost Czechoslovakia ... We retreat from Berlin? When Berlin falls, Western Germany will be next?'

US General L Clay, speaking in 1948

Source D

THE BIRD WATCHER

A cartoon from Punch, July 1948

Source E

'We demonstrated to the people of Europe that with their co-operation we would act ... resolutely when their freedom was threatened.'

President Truman: *Memoirs* (1955)

Specimen question

1 Read Source A (page 87). What evidence is there that fear may have driven the Soviet Union to blockade Berlin? Explain your answer. [5 marks]

Hints

Use your knowledge of events leading up to the blockade as well as the source. Who was the writer? Was he likely to have known the hopes and fears of the Soviet government? Had anything happened which might have led them to think that a strong German state was about to be set up?

Specimen question

2 What evidence is there in Sources B and C that the Western powers felt that they were forced to set up an air lift? Explain your answer. [5 marks]

Model answer

Attlee, who was British Prime Minister at the time, is quoted as saying that the Allies had 'no real choice' because otherwise they would have lost West Berlin. General Clay goes further. He thought that if, following the installation of a Communist government in Czechoslovakia, they lost West Berlin, then they would be turned out of Western Germany. These two opinions, one from the USA and one from Britain, are good evidence that both governments felt they had no choice, but had to mount the air lift.

Specimen question

3 What does Source D tell us about the Berlin air lift? To what extent is it backed up by the other sources? [8 marks]

Hint

The examiners realise that a cartoon like this may give different messages to different people. They will remember this when marking the answers. But to get good marks you need to link the points you make to details in the cartoon.

Model answer

The cartoon shows that Berlin received its supplies, even bulky, heavy items such as coal, from the air. It shows how vulnerable the air lift was. The aircraft, represented by the slow, delicate birds carrying their bundles, could easily have been shot down by the USSR, represented by Stalin, shown with his gun half-raised, as if in doubt what to do. This backs up the point made by Attlee in Source B that, at the time, people weren't absolutely sure that the Russians didn't want a showdown, so that the decision to use the air lift was risky.

Specimen question

4 What advantages did the Western Powers get out of the air lift? [4 marks]

Hint

Use your knowledge as well as the sources. What effect did the air lift have on the prestige of the USSR? Was this an advantage to the West?

Check

That you understand how the Communist takeover of Eastern Europe, the Truman Doctrine, the Marshall Plan and the Berlin blockade upset relations between the USSR and the West.

The Cuban Missile Crisis

In the autumn of 1962 the Soviet government, under Nikita Khrushchev, began to build missile sites in Cuba, and shipped nuclear missiles out to them.

Lead-up to the crisis timeline

1957 USSR launched Sputnik. Boost for USSR.

1958 Khrushchev threatened to hand Berlin over to East Germany as a 'free city'. Alarmed the West.

1959 Castro overthrew US-backed Cuban dictator. Asked for aid. USA refused, USSR agreed.

1961 Berlin Wall built. USSR more secure.

USSR sent man into space. Boost for USSR.

Bay of Pigs. Cuban exiles from USA landed on Cuba. Defeated. USSR stepped up aid.

Tip

Mini timelines like this (above) are a useful way of putting events in order briefly and clearly. Try to compile your own to help your revision.

Source B

'I decided to install missiles . . . with nuclear warheads in Cuba without letting the United States find out until it was too late to do anything about them. The missiles would stop the United States taking any action against Cuba.'

Nikita Khrushchev: *Khrushchev on Khrushchev* (1990)

Source C

'The presence of these large, long-range and clearly offensive weapons . . . constitutes an explicit threat to the peace and security of all the Americas . . . This action also contradicts the repeated assurances . . . that the Soviet Union had no need or desire to station strategic missiles on the territory of any other nation.'

US President Kennedy: Broadcast, 22 October 1962

Source D

'Your rockets are stationed in Turkey . . . Turkey lies next to us . . . Do you believe that you have the right to demand . . . the removal of such weapons that you qualify as offensive while not recognising the right for us?'

Nikita Khrushchev: Message to President Kennedy, 26 October 1962

Source A

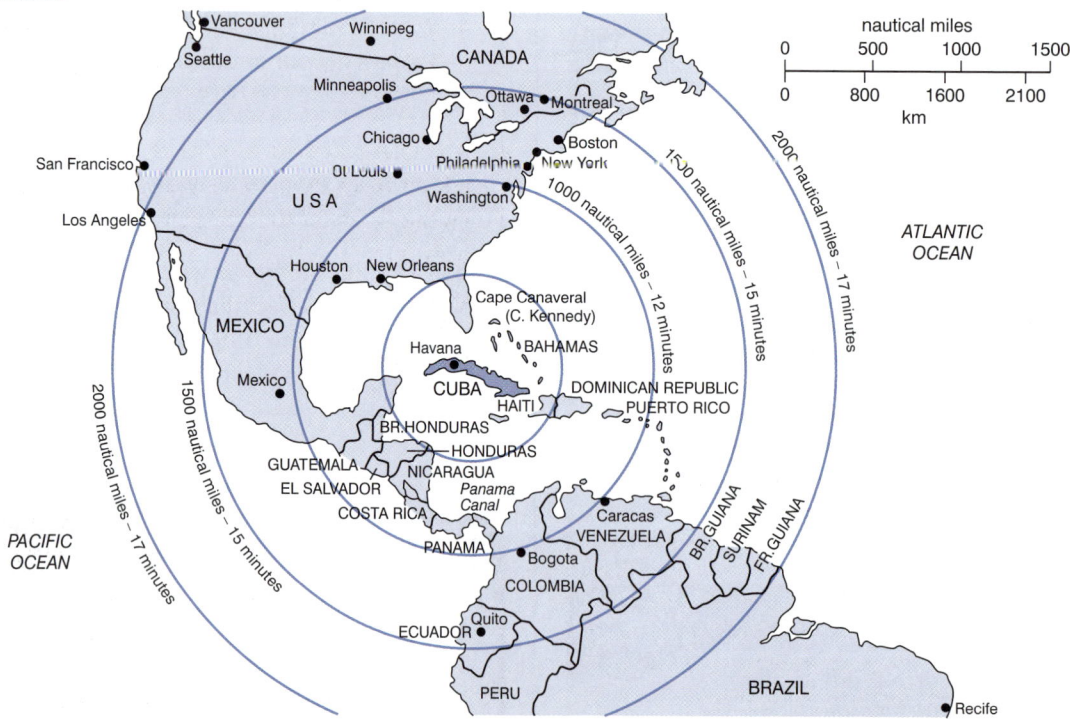

The area threatened by the missiles based in Cuba

Source E

'All ships of any kind bound for Cuba from whatever nation or port will, if found to contain cargoes of offensive weapons, be turned back ... We will call for the prompt dismantling and withdrawal of all offensive weapons in Cuba ... before the quarantine can be lifted.'

President Kennedy: Broadcast, 22 October 1962

Source F

'During the seventeen years that have passed since the end of World War 2 there has never been a more dangerous or closer confrontation of the major powers.'

U Thant, UN Secretary General: Statement to UN on 24 October 1962

Source G

'We sent the Americans a note saying we agreed to remove our missiles ... on condition that the President assured us that there would be no invasion of Cuba. Finally Kennedy gave in and agreed to [give] ... such an assurance. It was a great victory for us.'

Nikita Khrushchev: *Khrushchev on Khrushchev* (1990)

Source H

'In the Communist world [Khrushchev] suffered a blow to his prestige from which he was never really to recover. His judgement was called into question in every Communist capital including his own.'

Geoffrey Stern, Lecturer in International Relations: BBC documentary, 1985

Specimen questions

1 Why in 1962 might Khrushchev have felt confident enough to challenge Kennedy over Cuba?   [4 marks]

2 Why was President Kennedy alarmed that Khrushchev had placed missiles in Cuba?   [4 marks]

3 Is there good evidence in the sources that Khrushchev deliberately deceived Kennedy over his plans to put missiles in Cuba? Explain your answer.   [5 marks]

4 Could the Soviet rockets in Cuba be fairly compared with US rockets in Turkey? (Source D). Explain your answer.   [5 marks]

Hint

Remember you can use your own knowledge of the topic as well as the sources to answer this.

Specimen question

5 Why, do you think, did U Thant (Source F) think that the situation was so dangerous?   [3 marks]

Hint

Think of what might have happened as a result of the action outlined in Source E.

Specimen question

6 Why did President Kennedy take the steps outlined in Source E?   [10 marks]

Hint

The way to answer this question must depend on how many marks are on offer. A few marks demand a simple answer. Don't waste time giving more. But 10+ marks need careful thought.

If Kennedy had done nothing, what would the effects have been on his prestige in the USA, on the safety of the USA, on his allies, on the prestige of the USSR? If he had done more (e.g. sink the ships, bomb the missile sites), what might Khrushchev have done to retaliate? Nuclear war? So Kennedy compromised.

Specimen question

7 Khrushchev claimed that the Cuban Missile Crisis was 'a great victory' (Source G). So why did Geoffrey Stern (Source H) say it was a blow to his prestige? Explain your answer.   [10 marks]

Hints

Note the reason Khrushchev gives in Source B (page 90) for placing rockets in Cuba. Did he fulfil this aim? But was this his real aim? If it was not, then what was? Humiliation for the USA? Prestige for the USSR? Who backed down in the end?

Check

That you can explain why Khrushchev may have wanted to place rockets on Cuba, why Kennedy acted as he did, and what the results were.

The Vietnam War 1964–75

Background

Vietnam was part of Indo-China, which used to be a French colony. In 1954 the French were driven out by the Vietcong, a Communist guerrilla group. At the 1954 Geneva conference Indo-China was divided into four (*see* map). Laos and Cambodia were to be independent countries. North Vietnam, ruled by the Communists, and South Vietnam, ruled by a right-wing dictator, were to be united after free elections. Diem, the dictator supported by the USA, refused to hold elections. Why was the USA interested?

Source A

'We'd never heard of the place before . . . The country was absolutely blank on the whole subject of Vietnam. And therefore the more easily could we impose on it the ideas we had in mind about the Cold War and the necessity of fighting the evil of Communism.'

Professor Fairbank, a US foreign policy expert: BBC documentary, 1985

Source B

'If . . . Vietnam became . . . Communist . . . then it would probably be used as an effective base for further subversion outward and [surrounding countries] . . . would . . . tend to come under domination one at a time.'

Robert Bowie, US State Department official: BBC documentary, 1985

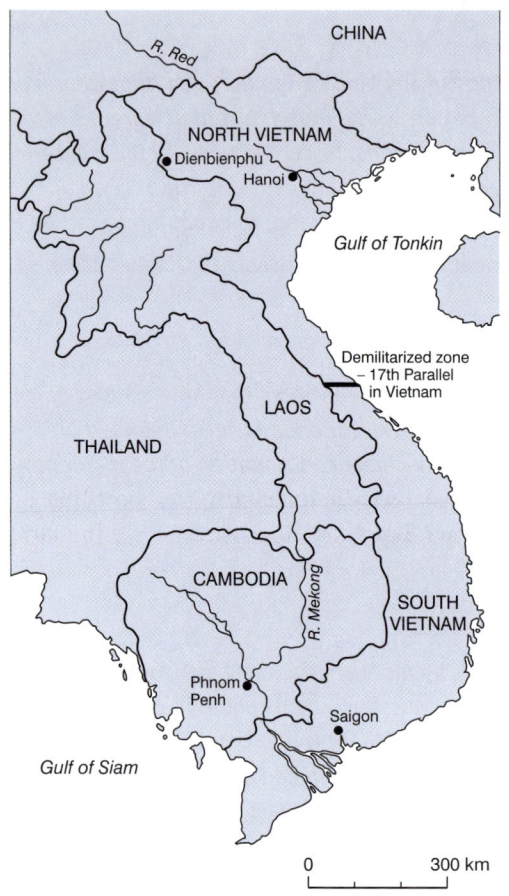

Indo-China in 1954

Source C

'The rulers in Hanoi are urged on by Peking. This is a regime which has destroyed freedom in Tibet, which has attacked India, and has been condemned by the United Nations for aggression in Korea. It is a nation which is helping the forces of violence in almost every continent.'

US President Lyndon Johnson: Speech, April 1965

Source D

'The Soviets were utterly opposed to free elections in Germany, utterly opposed to free elections in Korea, so . . . why should we accommodate them in one spot if they won't accommodate us in these other places?'

Dean Rusk, US Secretary of State: BBC documentary, 1985

Specimen question

1 Study the sources. Do they confirm the view that the US government had no interest in the welfare of the Vietnamese people? Explain your answer.   **[6 marks]**

Hints

This does not ask you just to list all the evidence which supports the view. You have also to look carefully for any evidence on the other side and weigh it against the rest.

Specimen question

2 The US government claimed that the war in Vietnam was a fight for democracy. Do the sources support this view? Explain your answer.   [6 marks]

Hint

Look particularly at Source D.

The development of the war

Vietnam timeline

1954–64	US aid to South Vietnam.
1964	Vietminh attacked US ships in Gulf of Tonkin. US sank Vietminh ships.
1965	US air raids on Hanoi. US sent troops to Vietnam.
1966	Over 150 US air raids a day on targets in North and South Vietnam.
1968	Tet offensive – Vietcong attacked nearly 100 towns in South Vietnam, 300 US deaths a week in Vietnam.
	US began air raids on Laos and Cambodia.
	Nixon reduced the number of US troops in Vietnam.
1972	Nixon promised to end war.
1973	Ceasefire signed. US troops withdrew.
1975	Vietcong took over South Vietnam.

Notes

- Total US casualties in Vietnam: 57,685 killed, 153,303 wounded.

- Vietnamese casualties: more than 2 million.

Source A

'JUST GIVE US THE TOOLS AND WE'LL GET THE JOB DONE'

Thurs., July 6, 1967   ST. LOUIS POST-DISPATCH

This cartoon, showing flag-draped US coffins, appeared in a US paper in July 1967

Source B

'Let us be proud of the two and a half million young Americans who served in Vietnam . . . with honour and distinction in one of the most selfless enterprises in the history of nations. And let us be proud of those who . . . gave their lives so that the people of South Vietnam might live in freedom.'

President Nixon: Speech, January 1973

Specimen questions

1 What effect was the cartoon intended to have on readers' attitude to the Vietnam War? [2 marks]

2 Was the cartoon's message accurate? Explain your answer. [4 marks]

3 Can President Nixon's view of the US role in Vietnam be justified? Explain your answer. [10 marks]

Hint

You earn good marks on questions like this by backing up the points you make with valid arguments and good evidence, no matter what view you take.

Model answer

President Nixon was right when he said that Vietnam was a 'selfless' war, because the USA had nothing to gain from it. The US government was fighting to prevent the Communists taking over South East Asia. Many US troops behaved bravely and honourably, but some committed atrocities, such as the Mi Lai massacre, and in any case some US tactics, such as the widespread use of napalm and defoliants, which were bound to damage innocent lives, were controversial. The US government never fought to enable the South Vietnamese to live in freedom. The governments the USA supported were right-wing dictatorships. When he spoke in 1973, on the occasion of signing the ceasefire, Nixon had to make an upbeat speech like this, but it is a very one-sided view.

Vietnam aftermath

The Vietnam War caused social conflict in the USA. The failure to prevent the Communist takeover made the USA lose confidence in itself.

Source

'If you want to, go ahead and fight in the jungles of Vietnam. The French fought there for seven years and still had to quit in the end. Perhaps the Americans will be able to stick it out a little longer, but eventually they will have to quit too.'

Khrushchev, in a conversation with Dean Rusk in 1961

Check

That you understand why, in spite of Khrushchev's warning, the USA got involved in the Vietnam War, and how Khrushchev's prophecy came true.

The Eastern Bloc 1953–89

Background

The Soviet Union controlled Eastern Europe through the Warsaw Pact, signed in 1955. It put all Eastern European armies under Soviet control, and allowed the USSR to station troops in Warsaw Pact countries, which shielded the USSR from an attack from the West (see map opposite).

In February 1956 the Russian leader, Khrushchev, made a speech criticising Stalin, who had died in 1953. He said:

'Stalin called people who did not agree with him "enemies of the people". This term allowed him to kill and imprison illegally anyone he wished. People couldn't argue with him.'

This speech made many people in Warsaw Pact countries believe that Khrushchev was in favour of reform and free speech.

The Hungarian Rising 1956

In October 1956 the Hungarian people overthrew their Stalinist leader, Rakosi, and set up Imre Nagy in his place.

Nagy's policies:
- the complete withdrawal of Soviet troops from Hungary
- local councils to replace Soviet power
- free elections
- improved justice system
- reform of police force
- farmland returned to private ownership
- Hungary to leave the Warsaw Pact
- to declare Hungarian neutrality in the Cold War.

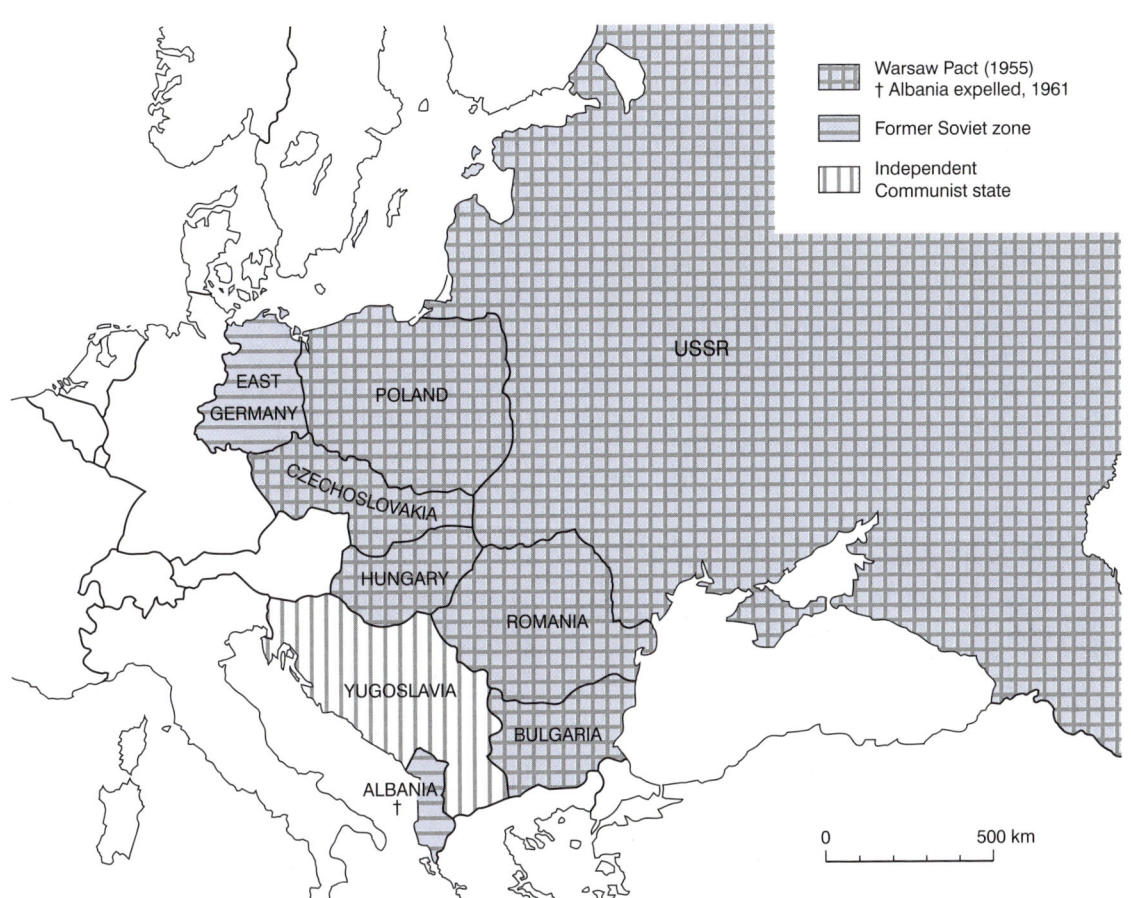

Warsaw Pact (1955)
† Albania expelled, 1961

Former Soviet zone

Independent
Communist state

Members of the Warsaw Pact, 1955

At first, Khrushchev supported Nagy, and promised to withdraw Soviet troops, but when Nagy said Hungary would leave the Warsaw Pact, Khrushchev sent Soviet tanks into Budapest, overthrew Nagy, and set up Janos Kadar in his place.

Specimen questions

1   What changes did Imre Nagy make in Hungary?   [4 marks]

2   Why did some of these changes upset the Soviet government?   [6 marks]

3   'The most important lesson of the Hungarian Rising of 1956 was that the Soviet Union was in complete control of its Eastern allies.' Do you agree with this statement? Explain your answer.
                                    [10 marks]

Hint

Always suspect phrases like 'most important'. For example, why was there a revolt in Hungary at all if the Soviets were in complete control? Why did Khrushchev allow some of Nagy's reforms? Would it be better to say that the Soviet Union was the final judge of what was acceptable? Another important lesson was that dissident Eastern Bloc countries could not expect any help from the West.

Check

That you can explain why some Eastern Bloc countries expected more freedom after 1953, and why the Soviet Union acted as it did against Hungary in 1956.

The Prague Spring 1968

In 1968 two new leaders, Alexander Dubcek and Ludovik Svoboda, took control of the Communist Party in Czechoslovakia. They brought in many reforms to areas such as the police, trade and travel.

1968 timeline

January	Dubcek became General Secretary of Czech Communist Party. Reforms began.
May–June	Soviet army manoeuvres on Czech borders. East German and Soviet press criticised reforms.
July	Meetings between Czech and other Warsaw Pact leaders.
4 August	Agreement reached. Reforms to go ahead.
14 August	Soviet press attacked reforms.
17 August	Brezhnev accused Dubcek of breaking agreement.
20 August	Soviet, East German, Hungarian, Polish and Bulgarian troops invaded Czechoslovakia.

Source A

'There was a tremendous discrepancy between the theory and the practice ... So I think all that we wanted to do, was to find a more honest, more human way to fulfil the aims we have in mind for the last twenty years.'

Y Hanzelka, Czech government spokesman, speaking in 1968

Source B

'The whole atmosphere was exciting. People were free to talk without fear of arrest and to make contact with new ideas, inside or outside Czechoslovakia.'

William Wallace: *Czechoslovakia*

Source C

'[A minister] reported ... that Soviet troops along with units from four other Warsaw Pact countries had crossed the borders into Czechoslovakia ... Dubcek said, "So they did it after all – and to me".'

Zdenck Mlynav, a Czech Communist Party official: *Night Frost in Prague*

Source D

'All the signposts, street names and name cards on apartment doors disappeared overnight. All the streets were called Dubcek or Svoboda Street. All the towns were named Dubcekov or Svobodov'

Ladislav Mnacko: *The Seventh Night*

Source E

'It was very hard coming down from the exhilaration of the changes. You suddenly found yourself completely helpless, crashing down to complete despair.'

Czech civilian looking back on 1968: BBC documentary, 1985

Specimen question

1 What evidence is there that Dubcek's government genuinely did not want to upset the Soviet Union? **[5 marks]**

Hints

Compare his reforms with those of Imry Nagy in Hungary in 1956. Look at the 1968 timeline. Look at Source C.

Specimen question

2 Is there any evidence that the USSR and its allies found it difficult to agree to invade Czechoslovakia? Explain your answer. **[4 marks]**

Hint

Look at the 1968 timeline.

Specimen questions

3 What evidence is there that the Czech people supported Dubcek's reforms? **[4 marks]**

4 Explain why the five powers eventually decided to crush the Czech reforms. **[6 marks]**

Hints

The answer to question 4 is not in the sources. Perhaps demand for reforms might spread? Might existing leaders lose power? Might Communism be undermined? Might the Warsaw Pact be undermined? Might the Warsaw Pact disintegrate? Was it too risky?

Check

That you understand why the USSR and its allies invaded Czechoslovakia.

The Prague Spring aftermath

The Soviet Union lost prestige. The Soviets were criticised by China, Albania and Romania as well as by all the Western powers.

The Berlin Wall

The USA, Britain and France controlled part of the city of Berlin and had the right to travel to it through East Germany. West Berlin was a shop-window for the West. It was very prosperous and had fewer restrictions than the East. What was more, it provided an easy route for East Germans who wanted to live in the West. The Soviet Union and East Germany tried to solve this problem in various ways (*see* timeline).

Specimen question

1 Why did the Soviet and East German authorities feel that they had to build the wall in 1961?   [4 marks]

Hint

To earn all four marks you will need to mention the particular circumstances of 1961.

Specimen question

2 What advantage did the wall give to the West?   [2 marks]

Berlin timeline

1948 USSR tried to force Western Powers out by blockade. Foiled by air lift.

1958 Khrushchev proposed to hand East Berlin over to the East Germans. West vetoed idea.

1959 140,000 East Germans left through West Berlin.

1960 200,000 East Germans left through West Berlin.

1961 **Jan–June** 100,000 East Germans left through West Berlin.

Khrushchev wanted to hand over all border controls to East Germans. West refused.

August Eastern forces built the Berlin Wall, sealing off West Berlin. West protested.

1963 President Kennedy visited Berlin. He said, *'There are those who say there is no difference between the East and the West. Let them come to Berlin.'*

Solidarity in Poland

Most Poles are Roman Catholics. They disliked the atheist Communist governments which had ruled them since 1948. Food was short and life was hard. In 1980 there were a number of strikes organised by Solidarity, a trade union led by Lech Walesa, an electrician. Solidarity signed an agreement with the government. In this agreement the government promised to increase food rations, reduce hours of work, allow freedom of worship and stop censoring the press and broadcasting.

Shortages continued in Poland and in the autumn of 1981 there were more strikes and demonstrations. Advised by the Soviet leader, Leonid Brezhnev, the Polish President, General Jaruzelski, dissolved Solidarity, arrested its leaders and imposed martial law. In 1983 Lech Walesa was awarded the Nobel Peace Prize.

Source

'If the outrages in Poland do not cease, we cannot and will not conduct business as usual with the perpetrators and those who aid and abet them.'

US President Reagan: Speech, December 1981

Specimen question

1   The USSR did not intervene in Poland in 1980. What message would this give to 'reformers' in Eastern Europe?

[3 marks]

Hint

Compare with the Prague Spring in 1968.

Specimen question

2   What did the USSR lose by its policy towards Poland in 1980 and 1981? Explain your answer.   [4 marks]

Hint

Was the policy consistent? Did it give an impression of strength and certainty?

Reform in the USSR 1985–89

In 1985 Mikhail Gorbachev became head of the Soviet government. He wanted to reform the Soviet system by introducing more economic competition and prosperity, less state control, and allowing the people to freely express their political opinions.

Gorbachev believed that the Soviet Communist Party was strong enough to remain in power after his reforms. He was wrong. The reforms resulted in the collapse of the whole Soviet system in the USSR.

Gorbachev's reforms also affected all the Communist states in Eastern Europe. Gorbachev made it clear that if the people there wanted a different system of government he would not try to prevent it. All the Communist governments were unpopular and inefficient, and in 1989 they all fell from power. Most important, the people of East Germany decided to join up with West Germany in a new united Germany.

Specimen question

Was Gorbachev responsible for the fall of Communism in Eastern Europe? Explain your answer fully.   [15 marks]

Hint

Always suspect statements that offer one simple explanation for things. Who appointed Gorbachev? Who helped him to carry out his policies? Why did the peoples of Eastern Europe want to get rid of their governments? Give examples of how they had tried in the past. Mention the growing uncertainty of Soviet policy.

Check

That you can explain why the USSR acted against Poland in 1981, why East Germans and the Soviet Union built the Berlin Wall and why the whole system collapsed in 1989.

The United Nations

The Second World War (1939–45) was incredibly destructive and expensive. World leaders were determined that there must never be another war like it. So in 1945 they set up the United Nations Organisation (UNO), which they hoped would help to keep the peace. They tried to make it stronger than the League of Nations had been.

Organisation

General Assembly Meets every year. Every member country has one vote. Discusses problems. Makes recommendations, appoints committees.

Security Council Five great powers are permanent members. Can veto decisions. Others selected by assembly for two years. Job is to preserve peace. Can order members to provide troops to keep the peace.

Central Organisation

Secretariat Administers UN under the control of the Secretary General, who can raise issues and suggest policies to the assembly and the Security Council.

Specimen question

1 In what ways was the United Nations stronger than the League of Nations had been?   [4 marks]

Hint

You need to use your knowledge about the League of Nations as well as the information given here.

Specimen question

2 Under what circumstances might the Security Council be unable to act, even though the majority of members wanted it to?   [2 marks]

More members

Since 1945 large numbers of former colonies have gained their independence and joined the UN.

> Source

'It used to be that the UN reflected the Cold War divisions which were mostly East–West. But . . . since about 1960 it has become . . . a forum for North–South encounters. . . . Now the big subjects are colonialism, sovereignty over natural resources and the evolution of the doctrine that the have-not nations "as a matter of right" are entitled to economic help from the have nations.'

David Popper, US Assistant Secretary of State: Speech, 1973

Specimen question

1 What evidence is there in the source that:
(a) before 1960 discussions in the UN Assembly were usually about political disagreements between Communist states and Western democracies
(b) after 1960 the Assembly was more interested in working for equality among the world's peoples?   [2 marks]

Hint

The purpose of this question is to check that you understand the source.

Specimen question

2 Do you think this source is reliable? Give reasons for your answer. [5 marks]

Hint

Should somebody in Popper's position have been familiar with what was going on in the UN? Might his view be biased? Might the representative of a 'have-not' country have had a different view?

The Korean War 1950–53

In 1950 Korea was divided into two. North Korea was Communist. South Korea was capitalist. Suddenly, without warning, North Korea invaded South Korea.

Source A

'I would be grateful . . . if your governments would consider the possibility of assistance . . . including combat forces [to repel the invasion].'

Trygve Lie, UN Secretary General: Letter to the Security Council, 1950

Source B

'What is happening . . . is important to every American . . . This attack has made it clear beyond all doubt that the international Communist movement is willing to use armed invasion to conquer independent nations.'

US President Truman: Speech, 1950

Source C

'If the aggressor gets away with it, aggressors all over the world will be encouraged. The same results which led to the Second World War will follow and another World War may result.'

Clement Attlee, UK Prime Minister: Speech, 1950

Specimen question

1 Do you think President Truman's claim regarding the 'international Communist movement' was justified? Explain your answer. [4 marks]

Hints

Was there such a thing as the 'international Communist movement'? Was North Korea acting with the advice and consent of China and the USSR?

Specimen question

2 What do you think Clement Attlee hoped to achieve by supporting Trygve Lie? [4 marks]

USSR boycott

When the invasion took place the USSR was boycotting the UN Security Council to protest against the fact that China's place on the Council had been given to the Nationalists, who only ruled Formosa, rather than the Communists, who ruled the whole of China.

In the absence of the USSR the Council agreed to Trygve Lie's request, and sixteen countries sent troops to Korea to fight against the North.

During the war 400,000 UN and 1.6 million Communist servicemen were killed or injured. Huge numbers of civilians were killed, injured and made homeless.

Korean War timeline

1950	June–Sept	Communist forces occupied all Korea except for an area around Pusan.
	Sept–Nov	UN troops drove North Korean forces back to the Chinese frontier.
	Nov	Chinese forces attacked the UN forces and drove them back into South Korea.
1951		UN forces drove Chinese back to about the 38th Parallel. Negotiations for armistice began.
1953		Armistice signed. Frontier between North and South fixed along the 38th Parallel.

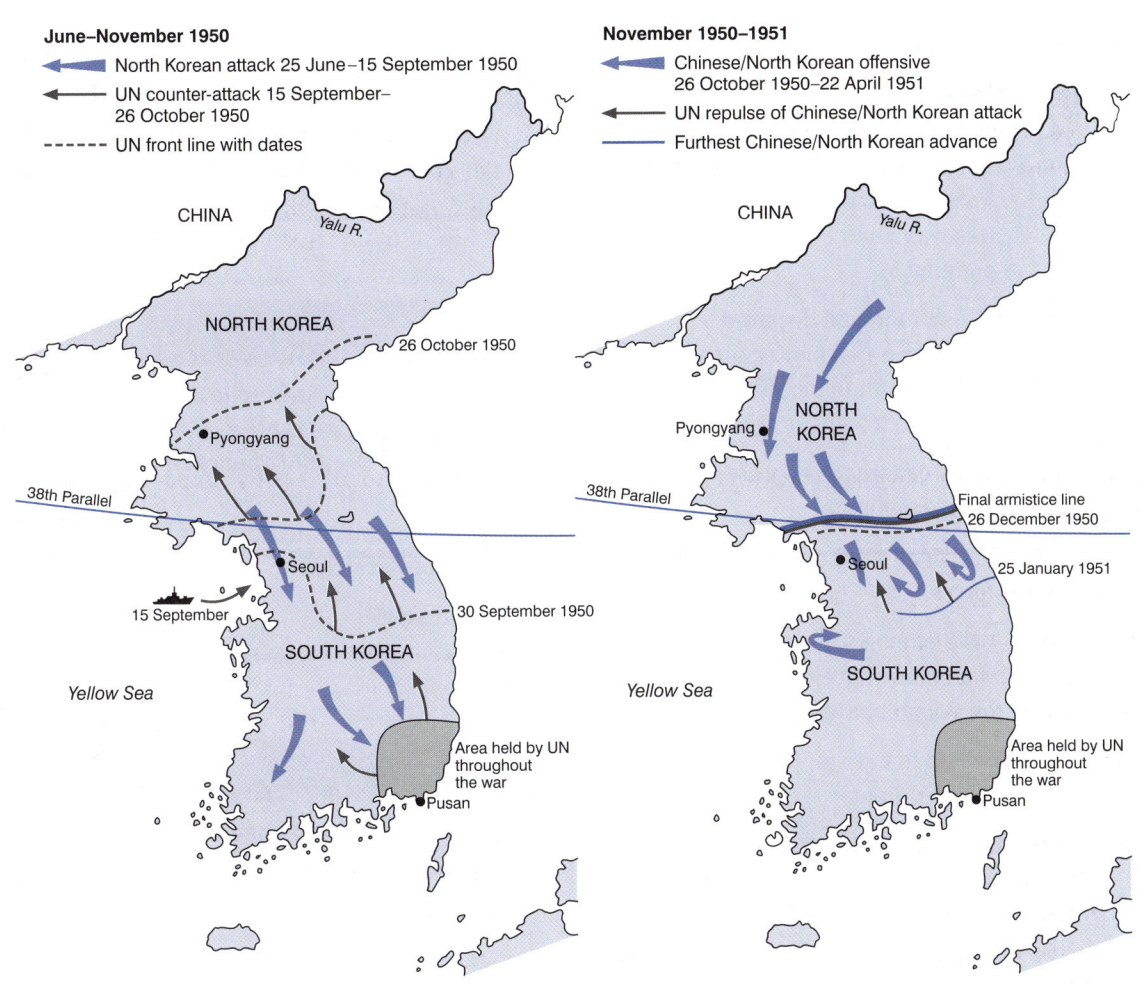

June–November 1950
- ← North Korean attack 25 June–15 September 1950
- ← UN counter-attack 15 September–26 October 1950
- - - - UN front line with dates

November 1950–1951
- ← Chinese/North Korean offensive 26 October 1950–22 April 1951
- ← UN repulse of Chinese/North Korean attack
- — Furthest Chinese/North Korean advance

Notes

The maps show what happened in visual form. Notice how much information can be crammed on to a map. Try drawing your own to help with your revision.

Hints

The North Koreans were driven back. But the quarrel between North and South was not settled. Action was possible only because the USSR was not present in the Security Council. The UN had to rely on a US general and the US army organisation. In the end the US took over the war. Conclusion?

Specimen question

Was the Korean War a success for the UN? Explain your answer. [10 marks]

The Congo Crisis 1960–65

Congo timeline

1960	**June**	Belgium granted Congo its independence under President Kasavubu and Prime Minister Lumumba.
	July	Moise Tshombe declared Katanga, a rich mining area, independent under his rule. The UN voted to send in troops.
1961	**Jan**	Katangan troops captured and killed Lumumba.
	Aug	Katangan troops attacked UN forces.
	Sept	UN Secretary General Hammarskjold killed in air crash on Congo border.
1963		Tshombe fled to Europe. Katanga reunited with Congo.
1964	**Jan**	UN forces left.
	July	Tshombe returned. Made Prime Minister. War continued.
1965		General Mobutu took control in a coup d'état.

Specimen question

How successful was the UN in the Congo? [6 marks]

Hints

Hammarskjold showed how the Assembly, where there was no veto, could bypass the Security Council. But what happened to the imposed settlement once the UN troops left? And how was the crisis eventually settled?

Conclusion?

Check

Go back over the section on the United Nations and draw a spider diagram on the organisation and work of the UNO.

Preview

What you need to know:

- **Problems caused by the breakdown of government in China after 1911**

- **How the Communists grew in strength and took over the country**

- **How Mao ruled China**

- **The changes which Deng introduced**

- **How China has dealt with the rest of the world**

Warning!

China is a vast country, containing a quarter of the world's population. Remember this whenever you read anything that deals with China as one unit. Remember, too, that the government has ruthlessly controlled the flow of information available both to Chinese citizens and to foreigners.

Notes

It is difficult to write Chinese names using the Western alphabet. This book uses the so-called Pinyin system, sometimes adding older versions in brackets.

China after the 1911 Revolution

Until 1911 China was governed by emperors. But in 1911 there was a rebellion and Yuan Shikai became president. He died in 1916. The new central government was very weak. Local warlords seized power in their own areas and fought each other to extend their territories.

Source A

'China was shredded by warlord wars. The peasants and labourers paid for these feudal wars in grain levies and in exorbitant taxes, for armies have to be paid and fed, and only China's peasantry – 90 per cent of the population – could do it. Armies also need recruits and only the peasantry could supply them. In some areas men were press-ganged while working the fields. In Szechuan province, taxes were levied seventy years in advance.'

Han Suyin: *The Morning Deluge* (1972)

Opposition to the warlords

There were two organisations which, combined, were strong enough to take on the warlords.

- **The Guomindang (Kuomintang) government**, headed by Sun Yixian (Sun Yat-sen), believed in democracy and socialism. Their army was commanded by Jiang Jiehi (Chiang Kai-Chek), who had trained as a soldier in Japan and the USSR.

- **The Communist Party,** who wanted to set up a Communist government. Most of them thought the best way to do this was to win the support of the industrial workers and take over the cities. One of the founders of the Party, Mao Ze Dong (Mao Tse-Tung), disagreed. He thought they ought to win over the peasants and control the countryside.

Source B

Execution in a Chinese street, 1927

China post-1911 timeline

1923 The Soviet government persuaded the Communists and the Guomindang to combine to suppress the warlords.

1925 Sun Yixian died. Jiang Jiehi took over as leader of the Guomindang.

1926 The combined forces took over most of northern China. Jiang, with the help of some warlords, decided to wipe out the Communists, and take complete control of the country.

1927 Mao, with fewer than 100 men, was driven into the hills.

Specimen questions

1 Study Source A on page 103. Why did many people in China welcome the United Front? **[5 marks]**

2 Look at Source B (page 103). It is a photograph taken in 1927. What does it show about conditions in Chinese towns at the time? **[5 marks]**

Hint

Remember it is one photograph taken in one town.

Check

That you understand the problems faced by China after 1911.

The Communists take over

Mao's army

Mao decided to recruit an army to defeat Jiang. He said: 'without a people's army the people have nothing . . . Political power grows out of the barrel of a gun'.

Source A

'Reading, writing, arithmetic were taught by officers to their men. The men sat on the ground tracing characters and figures in the dirt, since there were no paper or pencils. But the most powerful educational method consisted of . . . debate . . . Not only were battles and campaigns discussed, but the individual conduct of any commander could be criticised.'

Agnes Smedley: *Battle Hymn of China* (1944)

Source B

'He had a way of making even the enemy do what he wanted – he called it regaining the initiative. He would lead the enemy by the nose. He always did . . . He walked with us. He never used the stretcher we had prepared for him; he gave it to the wounded.'

Red Army soldier speaking of Mao, quoted in Han Suyin: *The Morning Deluge* (1972)

Source C

'Speak politely; buy at fair prices; return what you borrow; pay for what you damage; replace all doors and return the straw on which you sleep: dig latrines away from houses and fill them in when you leave; do not molest women, do not ill treat captives.'

Mao's rules for his army, 1927–28

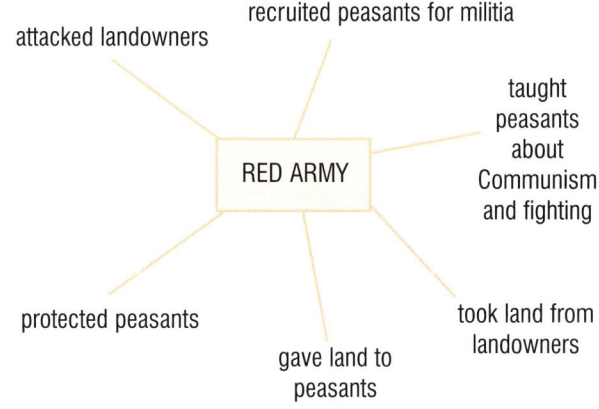

Specimen question

Using the information in the sources, explain why Mao's army became so powerful and popular. **[15 marks]**

Hints

Why might people have wanted to join the army? Why was Mao a popular commander? Why was the army popular in the countryside?

Check

That you understand how Mao organised his army.

The Long March

Jiang's army was much larger than the Red Army, and in 1934 he trapped the Red Army in Southern China. The Red Army broke out and marched to the North to establish a new base there.

Source A

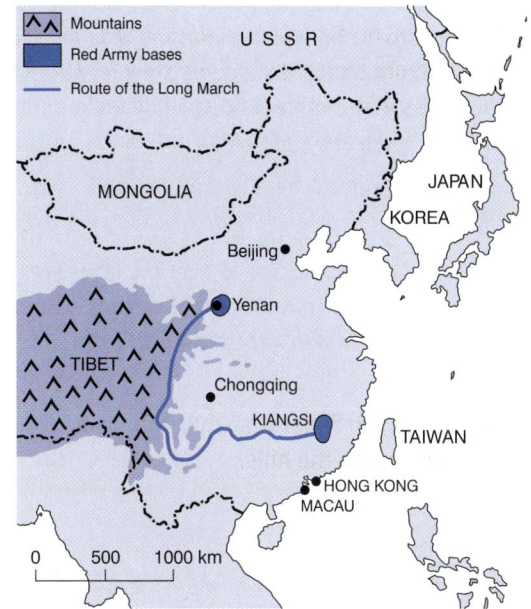

Source A

Specimen questions

1 Study the sources. Why did the Red Army take such a roundabout route? **[3 marks]**

2 The Long March added greatly to Mao's prestige. Why was that? **[10 marks]**

Hint

Use your own knowledge as well as the sources to answer this question.

Source B

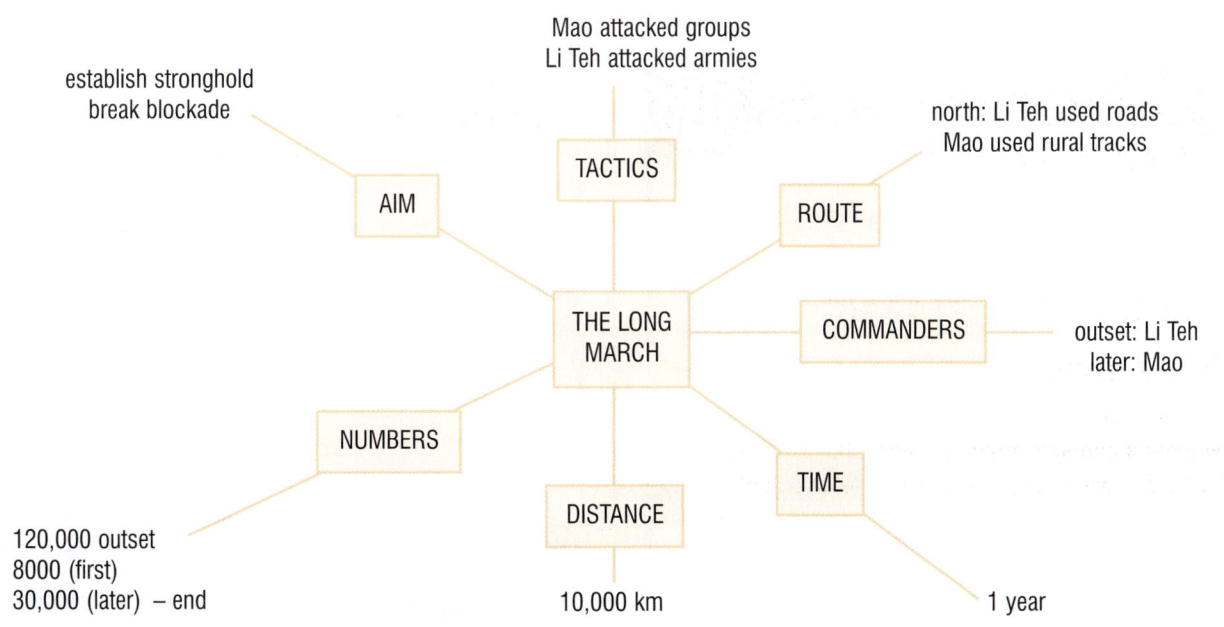

The war against Japan

In 1931 the Japanese had taken over Manchuria. By 1936 they were pushing further south. Jiang and Mao agreed to co-operate to drive them out. Mao's army fought in the north, Jiang's in the centre and south. Jiang fought pitched battles and usually lost. Mao did not.

Source A

'We must spread a guerrilla war all over the large areas occupied by the enemy, converting the enemy's rear into his front, and forcing him to fight ceaselessly throughout his occupied areas.'

Mao: Message to his army

Source B

'The enemy attacks, we retreat;

The enemy camps, we harass;

The enemy tires, we attack;

The enemy retreats, we pursue.'

Poem taught to Mao's army

Source C

'The Communist government and armies are the first in modern China to have positive and widespread popular support . . . because they are genuinely of the people.'

John Paton Davies: Official report to the US government, 1944

Japanese surrender

Gradually Mao drove the Japanese from the countryside. By 1945, when the Japanese surrendered, his army numbered 900,000 regulars and about 2 million militia. It controlled about 100 million people.

Specimen questions

1 Why would the Japanese army find it difficult to combat Mao's forces?
   [4 marks]

2 Explain why, in 1945, many Chinese people supported Communism.   **[10 marks]**

Hints

Associate it with: consideration for the poor, honesty, patriotism, success, efficiency? Remember to give examples.

The defeat of Jiang

After the defeat of the Japanese in 1945, Jiang, who had been supported and equipped by the USA, wanted to take over the whole of China. Mao refused, in spite of the fact that Jiang's army was five times as large as his. A new civil war broke out. By 1949 it was over. Jiang lost, and fled to Taiwan, where he set up his government.

Check

That you understand how and why Mao was able to take over the whole of China.

China under Mao

When Mao took over China he had a number of advantages. His reputation was of a hero and liberator and he had demonstrated to the people his confidence and imagination. He also had previous leadership experience as General and Governor and many supporters, including an army of 5 million and administrators such as Zhou Enlai.

He governed China through a council or committee, of which he was chairman. The day-to-day administration was controlled by the Prime Minister, Zhou Enlai.

Mao seemed to trust the Chinese people.

Source A

'More people mean a greater ferment of ideas, more enthusiasm and more energy. Never before have the masses of the people been so inspired, so militant and so daring as at present.'

Mao: Introducing a Co-operative (1958)

Source B

'Do not be afraid to make trouble. The more trouble you make and the longer you make it the better. Confusion and trouble always make an impact. They can clear things up.'

Mao: Advice to Party Members (1949)

Specimen question

Why might Zhou Enlai have disagreed with Mao's views? Explain your answer.
   [6 marks]

Hints

What was Zhou's job? Would more people, a 'ferment of ideas' and a lot of troublemakers make it easier or more difficult?

The early years 1950–53

Mao launched a series of campaigns to root out various 'evils' in Chinese life (*see* diagram below).

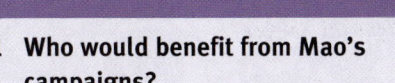

1950 'Three Mountains' against Feudalism, Capitalism and Imperialism.

1951 against counter-revolutionary landowners and capitalists. 250,000 executed.

Mao's campaigns

1952 'Three Antis' against corruption.

1953 'Five Antis' against profiteers.

Specimen questions

1 **Who would benefit from Mao's campaigns?** [3 marks]

2 **Who would enforce them?** [3 marks]

Hint

Use your own knowledge to answer these two questions.

Notes

Mao thought that collective farms would be big enough to afford machinery, fertilisers, etc. But the peasants disliked them. They wanted to own their own land. (Compare USSR.)

Source A

Production (million tonnes)			
	1952	**1957**	
		planned	**actual**
Coal	63.5	113.0	124.0
Iron	1.9	4.7	5.86
Steel	1.35	4.12	5.24
Oil	0.44	2.0	1.42
Cement	2.6	6.0	4.65
Power (billion kW)	7.26	15.9	19.1

The Five Year Plan 1953–57

As a rule China barely grew enough to feed its people and in bad years many starved. Industrial production was very low. Mao wanted to increase food production. He also wanted to make China into a great industrial power. The Five Year Plan was intended to achieve this. The main features of the Plan can be seen in the spider diagram below.

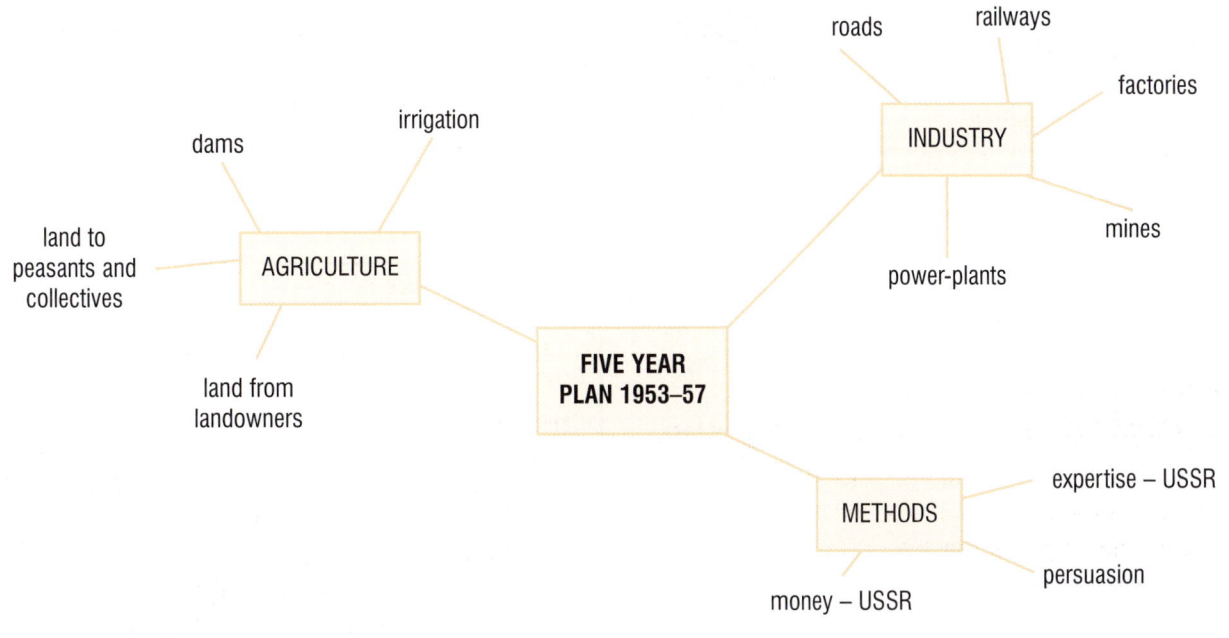

Source B

'Beijing was vivid . . . optimistic . . . Life had vastly improved.'

Alan Waddington: *Breakfast with Mao* (1986)

(Waddington was an English writer living in China in the 1950s.)

Specimen question

1 Study Source A (page 107). Are the figures quoted in it likely to be reliable? Explain your answer. [4 marks]

Hints

What do the figures show about the success of the Five Year Plan? Who would have compiled them? Were they likely to be biased? In any case would it have been possible to get accurate figures from such a vast country?

Specimen question

2 Is Source B good evidence of the success of the Five Year Plan? Explain your answer. [4 marks]

Hints

Might Waddington have been biased? Were conditions in Beijing necessarily typical of other parts of China?

The Great Leap Forward (1958–61)

Mao was not satisfied by the results of the Five Year Plan. He thought the people were hampered by officials. So he asked the people to tell him what they thought. He got a flood of complaints about collectivisation and high taxes, but no ideas which appealed to him. So he organised his Great Leap Forward, based on dividing the country into Communes.

Source A

'In this way industry, agriculture, commerce, education and military affairs can be combined thus making the task of leadership easier.'

Mao: Speech, 1958

Source B

A propaganda woodcut publicising the Great Leap Forward

Source C

'There was no food to eat in the village. The peasants were eating the leaves of trees, boiling leaves in water, mixing them with a little cornflour to make the leaves stick together.'

Chinese scholar quoted in Anne Thurston: *Enemies of the People* (1988)

Source D

Production statistics			
	1957	1960	
Grain	185	150	(million tonnes)
Cattle	50	42	(million head)
Sheep	52	50	
Pigs	145	82	

New policies

After the Great Leap Forward Mao lost some of his power. Prime Minister Zhou Enlai, President Liu Shaoqi and the Communist Party General Secretary Deng Xiaoping introduced new policies.

Encouraged people to set up their own businesses

Gave bonuses for increased output

Deng, Liu and Zhou's new policies

Grouped factories together and sent in technicians

Gave peasants their own plots of land

The Cultural Revolution

Mao hated the new reforms. He thought they were more like capitalism than communism. He feared that when he died the reformers would take over. So he decided to break them.

Mao knew he could rely on the army, and he was also supported by many students. He organised them into gangs of Red Guards, gave them copies of the Little Red Book of Quotations from Chairman Mao Zedong and told them to go out and rid the country of the 'Four Olds' – Old ideas, Old culture, Old customs and Old ways of life.

Source A

'[We vow to] apply sentence by sentence each of Chairman Mao's orders, even if we do not at first understand them.'

Oath taken by Red Guards

Source B

'Criticise ... all the representatives of the bourgeoisie [middle classes] who have infiltrated the party, the government, the army and the cultural world.'

Party instruction to students, 16 May 1966

Source C

'The leftists ordered ... criticism sessions in the courtyards of the houses of Liu and of Deng Xiaoping ... Liu and [his wife] were struck and kicked and made to sit in unbearably uncomfortable positions ... The session lasted over two hours. Liu's face was bruised and swollen.'

Beijing Workers' Daily (1980)

Note: Liu and Deng were both disgraced. Liu disappeared and died. Deng had to work as a labourer for several years.

Source D

'I saw rows of teachers ... with black ink poured over their heads and faces ... They all wore dunces' caps ... Hanging from their necks were buckets filled with rocks.'

Ken Ling: *Red Guard: From Schoolboy to Little General* (1972)

Source E

'Red Guards ... have caused work stoppages in the factories and the countryside by persuading workers and peasants that it is more important to intervene elsewhere than to work.'

Beijing Revolutionary Committee, 1967

Specimen questions

1 **Who were the Red Guards?**
[4 marks]

2 **What justification did they think they had for attacking (a) the teachers and (b) President Liu and Deng?** [5 marks]

Specimen question

3 **What evidence is there in the sources that the Red Guards disrupted:**
   (a) the government
   (b) industry and agriculture
   (c) the educational system? [6 marks]

Hint

Look at Sources A and B.

Hint

Beware! How general is the evidence in the sources?

The results of the Cultural Revolution

The spider diagram will remind you of the results of the Cultural Revolution. Even Mao was alarmed by the results of the Cultural Revolution. He had to use the army to disband the Red Guards. By the end of 1968 order had been restored.

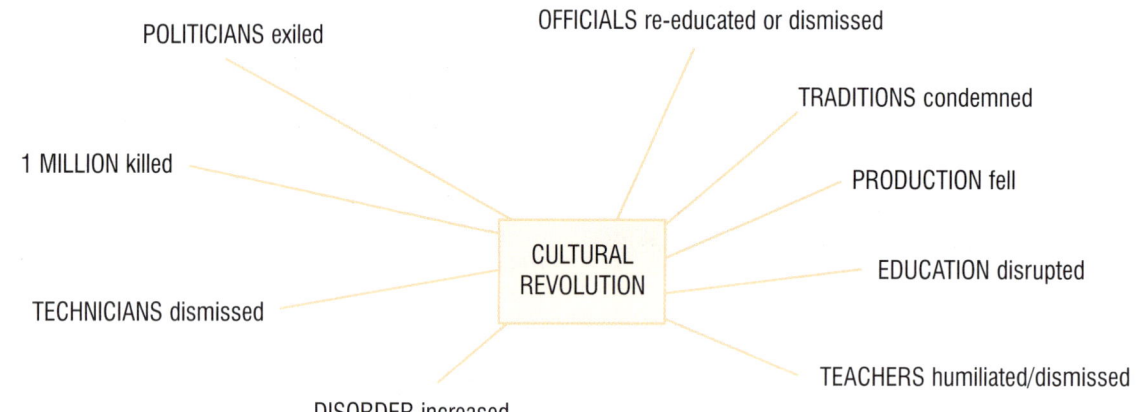

POLITICIANS exiled

OFFICIALS re-educated or dismissed

TRADITIONS condemned

1 MILLION killed

PRODUCTION fell

TECHNICIANS dismissed

CULTURAL REVOLUTION

EDUCATION disrupted

TEACHERS humiliated/dismissed

DISORDER increased

Check

That you understand the aims and results of the Cultural Revolution.

Mao's last years 1968–76

After 1968 Mao relied on Zhou Enlai and, after he had been reinstated in 1973, Deng Xiaoping. They thought that China needed a few years' peace and stability to recover from the Cultural Revolution. Mao's wife, Jiang Qing, and several other left-wing Communists did not agree. They wanted further reforms and tried to discredit Zhou and Deng. In 1976 Zhou and Mao both died. Jiang and three of her supporters – The Gang of Four – were arrested and imprisoned. By the middle of 1977 Deng had taken complete control.

Check

Your opinion of Mao. What were his strengths and his weaknesses?

China under Deng 1977–90

As a result of the policies of Deng's government (*see* diagram below), production increased. Farmers and businessmen made money.

Farmers had to produce a quota for the community and kept the rest.

He encouraged foreigners to visit China and invest their money.

He increased the output of consumer goods.

Deng's policies

Factories had to produce a quota. Workers earned bonuses for extra.

He tried to limit the size of Chinese families.

He insisted that Communist Party rule continued.

He replaced elderly officials by young people.

Source A

'The main job of socialism is to increase production, steadily improve the life of the people and keep making society richer.'

Deng Xiaoping: Speech, 1986

Source B

'The colour of the cat does not matter so long as it catches the mouse.'

Deng Xiaoping: Saying

Source C

'In their heady pursuit of personal profit, many villagers ... [help] themselves to all kinds of public property ... There is more theft, more squabbling over land use and water.'

Lynn Pan: *The New Chinese Revolution* (1988)

Specimen question

1 Why did Deng introduce new policies after 1977? Explain your answer fully. **[15 marks]**

Hint

This question demands a lot of explanation. You need to explain how Mao's policies – particularly the Cultural Revolution – had failed, and how Deng hoped that his new, more practical policies (say what they were) would improve matters.

Specimen question

2 How could Deng's policies be blamed for the anti-social activities described by Lynn Pan (Source C)? **[4 marks]**

Tiananmen Square 1989

Deng Xiaoping kept tight control of the Chinese Communist Party.

In 1987 he dismissed the party chairman, Hu Yaobang (b. 1915), because he wanted more reforms than Deng thought right.

In 1988 Deng abolished price controls. Prices rose. There were riots. Deng reinstated controls.

In 1989 Hu Yaobang died, and a huge number of students gathered in Tiananmen Square in Beijing to mourn him and demand democratic reforms. The students and their supporters occupied the square for several weeks, in spite of being ordered to disperse. In the end armed troops with tanks cleared the square and the surrounding streets, killing hundreds of demonstrators. Later, thousands were arrested and imprisoned.

Source A

'The wrong man has died ... Those who should die still live. Those who should live have died.'

'China still has an emperor without an emperor's title, a senile and fatuous autocrat ... Down with autocracy ... Rule by old men must end.'

Student slogans in Tiananmen Square

Source B

'A serious counter-revolutionary rebellion has broken out in the capital. The People's Liberation Army has been restrained for some days. However the counter-revolutionary rebellion must now be resolutely counter-attacked.'

Army proclamation in Tiananmen Square, 2 am June 4 1989

Source C

'As bodies crumpled to the ground, the crowd behind them scattered . . . The army delivered a finale of machine gun fire from armoured troop carriers. Then, for a moment the avenue was still: a hundred yard length of corpses, abandoned bicycles and prone, terrified survivors. That first drama would repeat itself many times during the day.'

Fathers and Higgins: *Tiananmen* (1989)

(The authors were British journalists in Beijing in 1989.)

Specimen question

1   Why did the Chinese government decide to crush the demonstrators in Tiananmen Square? Explain your answer fully.   [10 marks]

Hints

This is to some extent a matter of opinion, so if you can make a good case for your view, you will get good marks. You might consider: threat to party rule – students' contempt for Deng and authority – back to the days of the Cultural Revolution? Deng's and the country's sufferings in the Cultural Revolution remembered? Remember to back up what you say by examples from the sources and your own knowledge.

Specimen question

2   Why did the government hesitate so long before sending the troops in?   [5 marks]

Hints

Remember Mao's quote in 1949: 'Do not be afraid to make trouble.' Should they use the army to crush people 'making trouble'? Remember the number of foreign correspondents in Beijing. What effect would using the army have on public opinion abroad? Refer to Source C. Why did foreign opinion matter?

Check

That you understand what Deng was trying to do and why he crushed the students in Tiananmen Square.

China and the outside world 1949–90

Chinese borders

The Chinese revolutionary government claimed all the territory traditionally ruled by the emperors. The timeline opposite shows the main areas lost by China, and what Communist governments have done to resolve the problems.

Specimen question

Have the Chinese Communists been aggressive towards their neighbours? Explain your answer.   [10 marks]

Hint

What does 'aggressive' mean? Could the Chinese claim they were only trying to get back and protect their own? How might that seem to their neighbours? Remember to give examples to illustrate your general points.

Timeline

Mongolia	Taken by Russia in 1911. Became independent Mongolian People's Republic in 1924.	Sino-Soviet Treaty guaranteed independence in 1950. Border with China agreed in 1987.
Macao	Seized by Portugal in 1511.	Chinese took over in 1999.
Hong Kong	Taken over by Britain 1841–98.	Chinese took over in 1997. Capitalist system guaranteed for 50 years.
Tibet	Became independent of China under British influence in 1911.	China reoccupied Tibet in 1950.
Taiwan	Occupied by Japan in 1895. Jiang Jiehi (Chiang Kai-Chek) took over in 1945.	China offered the same terms as for Hong Kong. No agreement.

Wars on China's borders

Korea	**1950**	China invaded Korea when General MacArthur threatened to cross the Yalu River into China.
India	**1962**	China accused India of supporting a rebellion in Tibet. Invaded India, defeated Indian forces and then withdrew.
USSR	**1969**	Following various border disputes, Chinese and USSR troops clashed on the Ussuri River.

China and the USSR

At first China was on good terms with the USSR, and relied on Russian help to build up industry and agriculture.

But Mao distrusted the Russians. He disagreed with their policy of peaceful co-existence with the West, and disapproved of the invasion of Czechoslovakia. So he openly criticised the Soviet government. In addition there were frequent border disputes, so relations between the two countries deteriorated.

China and the USA

After the Second World War the US government still recognised Jiang Jiehi as rightful ruler of China, even though he had been driven out to Taiwan. Mao feared that the USA wanted to overthrow the Communist government. He thought there would probably be a nuclear war between East and West. He invaded Korea when American troops threatened the Chinese frontier in 1950 and helped Communist forces in Vietnam to fight against the USA.

In 1971 President Nixon agreed to recognise the Communists as rightful rulers of China, and in 1972 he visited Beijing. Mao said it was '*a tactical alliance with a secondary enemy to defeat a primary one [the USSR]*.'

Specimen question

What would you expect the following people to think of Nixon's visit to Beijing:

(a) a member of Jiang Jiehi's government on Taiwan

(b) a Communist who supported the USSR

(c) a US businessman who wanted to trade with China?

Explain your answers. [10 marks]

Check

That you understand China's attitude to the rest of the world.

Preview

What you need to know:

- Why the Liberals introduced social reforms, and the part played by social reformers like Rowntree and by politicians like Winston Churchill and Lloyd George

- How children, old people, ill and unemployed workers were helped, and how effective the reforms were

- Why women did not have the vote at this time, the differences between the NUWSS and the WSPU, why and how the suffragettes broke the law and how the government reacted

- In what ways the government increased its powers in the First World War, and how it made use of censorship and propaganda

- The part played by women in the First World War and why the 1918 Representation of the People Act was passed

The Liberal reforms

Why were they introduced?

In the past most people believed that if you were poor it was your own fault. Social reformers like Seebohm Rowntree did research in York into the real causes of poverty. This is what he found:

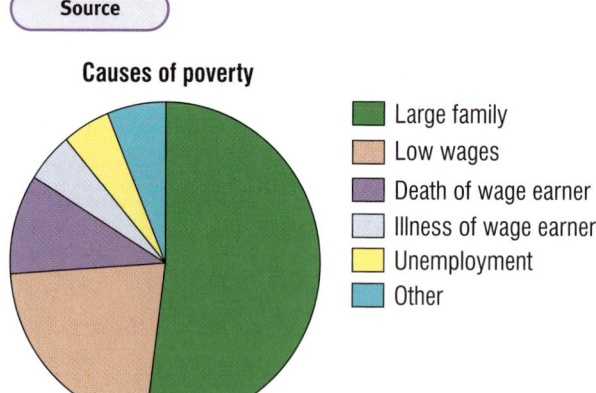

Source

Causes of poverty

- Large family
- Low wages
- Death of wage earner
- Illness of wage earner
- Unemployment
- Other

Specimen question

Why would Rowntree's findings lead to a change in government policy?   [5 marks]

Hint

How many of the items on Rowntree's list were not the fault of the poor? And if the poor were not to blame for poverty, it was up to the state to get involved in helping them.

The Liberals won the 1906 election with a huge majority. From 1906 to 1914 they set about a massive programme of social reform intended to help millions of poor people: children, old people, workers and the sick. They used the state to improve people's lives in a way that had never been done before, marking the beginning of the 'Welfare State'.

Reasons for social reform

- **Key individuals**
  Winston Churchill and David Lloyd George became convinced that the state had to step in to help the poor.

- **The Boer War 1899–1902**
  In some areas over half the recruits called up to fight in the Boer War had been too unfit to fight. How could Britain be a successful imperial power if its people were unfit to fight?

- **Rivals**
  Britain was being overtaken as an industrial nation by Germany. German workers had a good system of social welfare.

- **Socialism**
  Working-class movements were getting stronger. The new Labour Party won 29 seats in 1906. The Liberals were afraid they would lose working-class votes to Labour if they didn't do something to help working people.

What did the Liberals do?

Date	Children	Old people	Workers	Illness and unemployment
1906	School meals started			
1907	School medicals to check the health of children			
1908	Children's Charter: different treatment from adults at law		8-hour day for miners	
1909		Old Age Pensions: single person 25p, married couple 37.5p if over 70 and on an income of less than 60p a week	Labour Exchanges	
1910			Half-day off for shop workers	
1911				Insurance schemes set up by National Insurance Act. Illness: Every worker earning under £3 a week paid 2p a week. Employer added 1.5p, government 1p. If ill, worker could claim 50p a week for 26 weeks. Unemployed: Worker, employer and government paid 1p a week. If unemployed, worker could claim 35p a week for up to 15 weeks.

Specimen question

What difficulties did the Liberals have in getting the 1911 Insurance Act passed and how did they eventually succeed?   [8 marks]

Hint

Why were the Conservatives so opposed to the Act? How did they use the House of Lords to block it? How did the Liberals get past the House of Lords?

Some criticisms of these reforms

- Payments were not much – a 'lifebelt'. They were not meant for people to live on.
- Payments did not last long. In the 1930s Depression some workers were unemployed for several years.
- Only the (usually male) breadwinner was helped. There was no health care for other members of the family, especially women, who might need it more.

BUT the reforms did make a start, especially in caring for children and old people.

Check

That you know how different groups of people were helped by these reforms and what was so new about them.

Women and the vote

For most of the nineteenth century, women were believed to be inferior to men. By the end of the century attitudes had begun to change. However, although by this time about 60 per cent of men in Britain could vote, women could not. Why was this? Opinion was divided (*see* table below).

Votes for women

FOR	AGAINST
• Parliament's decisions affect both men and women • Women are now showing that they are equal to men at work and in education • Women can vote in local elections. Many women are councillors and mayors • Women pay taxes just as men do. They should have a say in how the money is spent • Educated women cannot vote, while uneducated men can	• Women are home-makers; men should take the decisions in the outside world • Women are emotional, not rational • Politics is a dirty business which women are too pure to mess about with • If women go into politics they will neglect their families • Women do not fight in wars, so do not earn the right to vote • The 60 per cent of males who vote are the better off and better educated. If women are given the vote on the same basis, the Conservatives will get more support

Source

'Mother would teach, by action and words, that girls and women should submit to husbands and brothers. Their duty was to feed them well, run their errands and bear all burdens except physical ones.'

Joseph Ashby, describing his nineteenth-century childhood in his autobiography

Specimen question

By 1900 the attitudes described in Source A were changing. How were changes in:

(a) women's education

(b) the law

(c) new technology jobs

affecting the position of women at this time?

[7 marks]

Suffragists and suffragettes

Source A

'Bad laws made without due authority ought not to be obeyed, but ought to be resisted by every honest man and woman. It is such laws that militant suffragettes have broken.'

Christabel Pankhurst, WSPU leader

Source B

'I hate militancy, as do the majority of suffragists. None of the triumphs of the women's movement has been won by physical force.'

Millicent Fawcett, NUWSS leader, in 1908

Source C

THE SHRIEKING SISTER.

The Sensible Woman. "YOU HELP OUR CAUSE? WHY, YOU'RE ITS WORST ENEMY!"

A cartoon published in *Punch* in 1906

Notes

• 1897 NUWSS National Union of Women's Suffrage Societies 'Suffragists'
• 1903 WSPU Women's Social and Political Union 'Suffragettes'

Specimen question

What were the differences between the suffragists and the suffragettes?

[10 marks]

Hints

This number of marks requires quite a full answer – at least a page. Look for as many differences as you can. The main one, of course, is over tactics, as the sources show, but there are others. The suffragists were a much larger, older organisation, dedicated to peaceful action. The suffragettes were only founded in 1903, out of frustration at the apparent lack of success of the suffragists.

Suffragette actions

In 1911 the Liberals seemed about to give women the vote, but then suddenly dropped the idea.

- **Suffragists** had a meeting with the Prime Minister to try to persuade him to change his mind.
- **Suffragettes** interrupted political meetings, shouting 'Votes for Women!' and throwing eggs at politicians, smashed shop windows, set light to letter-boxes, slashed paintings in art galleries and dug up the greens on all-male golf courses. One suffragette, Emily Wilding Davison, tried to grab the rein of the King's horse at the Derby in 1913 and was killed.

Source A

'The woman rushed from the rails as the horses rounded Tattenham Corner. She did not interfere with the racing but she nearly killed a jockey as well as herself and she brought down a valuable horse. A deed of this kind is unlikely to increase the popularity of the women's cause.'

The Times (6 June 1913)

Source B

'The procession was watched by dense crowds. Nearly five thousand members from all over the country marched in undisturbed quiet and orderliness behind the coffin.'

The *Manchester Guardian,* reporting on the funeral of Emily Wilding Davison

Specimen question

Compare the reactions of these two newspaper accounts to the death of Emily Wilding Davison.

[5 marks]

Hint

Look for the underlying attitudes of each newspaper account. How sympathetic to Emily Wilding Davison is each one?

Model answer

These two sources obviously have very different views of the death of Emily Wilding Davison. Source A shows her no sympathy and seems more concerned about the horse and the jockey. The paper seems irritated by her action and does not think it will do anything to win women the vote.

Source B, on the other hand, is impressed by the funeral procession. It reports the large size of the crowd and the 'undisturbed quiet and orderliness' of the procession. Whatever the paper's views of votes for women, all this creates a good impression of the suffragettes.

Reactions to the suffragettes

Suffragettes were put in prison for their violent acts. They went on hunger strike and the government forcibly fed them. Then the Cat and Mouse Act 1913 was passed. This allowed the government to release suffragettes, let them recover a little and then re-arrest them.

When war broke out in 1914 women still did not have the right to vote.

Check

That you understand why women campaigned for the vote in different ways.

The Home Front in Britain during the First World War

Home Front timeline

1914	**4 Aug**	Britain declared war on Germany.
	8 Aug	Defence of the Realm Act (DORA) passed.
	16 Dec	First British civilians killed when German warships shelled Hartlepool, Whitby and Scarborough.
1915	**19 Jan**	First Zeppelin air raids.
	autumn	Government set up its own munitions factories, many employing lots of women, owing to a shortage of male workers. Government made agreement that women should be allowed to work with men on the same pay only as long as the war lasted.
1916	**25 Jan**	Conscription introduced for all single men aged 18–40.
	16 May	Conscription extended to married men.
	1 July	First day of Battle of the Somme.
	Aug	British propaganda film *The Battle of the Somme* shown in cinemas.
	7 Dec	Lloyd George became Prime Minister.
1917	**Feb**	Women's Land Army formed.
	April	German U-boats sank one in four British merchant ships. Food supplies running low.
	Nov	Voluntary rationing scheme introduced: failed.
1918	**11 Nov**	Armistice (ceasefire). War over.
	14 Dec	General election: women over 30 and some women over 21 given right to vote for the first time.

Recruiting

British military planners had always assumed that a war would be short, so the British Army in 1914 was small. After only a few weeks it became clear that this war could go on for years. Britain would need a large army. For the time being soldiers of the Indian Army filled the gap, and a huge recruitment campaign was started, led by Lord Kitchener. Young men were put under great pressure to join up. (*See* Chapter 1.)

> **Source A**

'They asked my height and I told them. They hummed and haaed about it. I'm five foot six with paper stuffed into my shoes. Anyway, I says to them, "There's six of my pals joining up, all footballers". So they says, "Aw, go on, let him in". So I was one of the Midgets.'

Charlie Taylor, describing how he joined up

> **Source B**

A 1914 recruitment poster

> # REMEMBER SCARBOROUGH!
>
> The Germans who brag of their "CULTURE" have shown what it is made of by murdering defenceless women and children at SCARBOROUGH.
>
> But this only strengthens
>
> # GREAT BRITAIN'S
>
> resolve to crush the
>
> # GERMAN BARBARIANS
>
> # ENLIST NOW!

A 1915 recruitment poster

Specimen question

How were people persuaded to volunteer to become recruits in the British Army in the First World War? [6 marks]

Conscription and conscientious objectors

By the end of 1915 the flow of volunteers had slowed down, but the number of soldiers killed and injured was high. In January 1916 conscription was introduced.

Some people refused to fight. They said their consciences would not let them, so they were called conscientious objectors ('COs' or 'conchies'). Some had religious reasons for refusing to fight, some had political reasons. They were often treated badly.

Source A

'Out of the darkness we salute our working class comrades of every land. Across the roar of guns we send greetings to German Socialists – they are no enemy of ours, but our faithful friends.'

Proclamation from the Independent Labour Party, 1914

Source B

'I think you are exploiting God to save your own skin. A man who would not help to defend his own country is a coward and a cad. You are nothing but a shivering mass of unwholesome fat.'

Councillor at Shaw, Manchester, interviewing conscientious objectors, 1916

Specimen question

Why were many people in Britain so hostile to conscientious objectors in the First World War? [8 marks]

Hint

You will need to bring in here your knowledge of the war itself – the high casualties, conditions in the trenches, etc.

DORA (The Defence of the Realm Act) 1914

This Act gave the government huge, sweeping powers. They could take over land and factories, introduce censorship. People could be arrested for:

- talking about navy or army matters in public
- spreading rumours
- trespassing on railway bridges or tracks
- buying binoculars
- feeding bread to dogs, chickens or horses during the food shortage
- using invisible ink when writing to someone abroad.

The government introduced:
- British Summer Time (putting the clocks forward in summer to allow more work to be done in factories by daylight)
- weaker beer and pub licensing hours.

Source A

'If the people really knew [the truth about the war] the war would be stopped tomorrow. But of course they don't – and can't – know. The reporters don't write it and the censors wouldn't pass the truth.'

Lloyd George, in a private conversation with a newspaper editor, December 1917

Source B

DEFENCE OF THE REALM. E.P. 6.

MINISTRY OF FOOD.

BREACHES OF THE RATIONING ORDER

The undermentioned convictions have been recently obtained:—

Court	Date	Nature of Offence	Result
HENDON - -	29th Aug., 1918	Unlawfully obtaining and using ration books -	3 Months' Imprisonment
WEST HAM -	29th Aug., 1918	Being a retailer & failing to detach proper number of coupons	Fined £20
SMETHWICK -	22nd July, 1918	Obtaining meat in excess quantities - - -	Fined £50 & £5 5s. costs
OLD STREET -	4th Sept., 1918	Being a retailer selling to unregistered customer	Fined £72 & £5 5s. costs
OLD STREET -	4th Sept., 1918	Not detaching sufficient coupons for meat sold -	Fined £25 & £2 2s. costs
CHESTER-LE-STREET	4th Sept., 1918	Being a retailer returning number of registered customers in excess of counterfoils deposited - - - -	Fined £50 & £3 3s. costs
HIGH WYCOMBE	7th Sept., 1918	Making false statement on application for and using Ration Books unlawfully - - - - - - -	Fined £40 & £6 4s. costs

Enforcement Branch, Local Authorities Division,
MINISTRY OF FOOD.
September, 1918.

Government poster, 1917

Specimen question

How did the British government use propaganda and censorship in the First World War? **[10 marks]**

Hint

Think about both sides of this question: propaganda to persuade people to do and believe certain things, censorship to stop them knowing certain things. Find good examples of each.

A ten-mark question requires a full answer, not a brief one. Make a plan so that your answer has several paragraphs.

Check

That you understand the many different ways that the war affected everyone's lives in Britain.

Women and the First World War

As soon as the war started, women called off their campaign for the vote and threw their energies into the war effort. They supported Kitchener's recruitment drive, knitted socks for soldiers and sent cigarettes and chocolates to the trenches.

As more and more men joined the armed forces, there was soon a desperate shortage of labour: Britain was 2 million workers short by 1916. Women stepped into the breach.

Source A

'At this hour of England's need, I do hereby pledge myself in the name of the King and the country to persuade every man I know to offer his services to the country, and I also pledge myself never to be seen in public with any man who, being fit for service, has refused to respond to his country's call.'

Oath taken by women members of the Active Service League

Source B

A 1915 recruitment poster

Source C

Job	Women workers	
	1914	**1918**
Munitions	212,000	947,000
Transport	18,200	117,200
Commerce	505,200	934,500
Agriculture	190,000	228,000
Government and teaching	262,000	460,200
Hotels and catering	181,000	220,000
Industry	2,178,600	2,970,600
Domestic service	1,658,000	1,250,000
Self-employed	430,000	470,000
Nurses and secretaries	542,000	652,000

Specimen question

What kinds of jobs did women do in the First World War?   [10 marks]

Model answer

The table (Source C) shows that the number of women increased in almost every field of employment. Nearly 2 million more women were in employment by 1918 than had been in 1914. Some of the jobs women did were traditional: cooking, cleaning, nursing. They also moved easily into clerical jobs in offices. As the war went on they took jobs they had never done before: driving buses, delivering coal, digging graves. Some got quite close to the fighting as front-line nurses.

The greatest increase in numbers of women employed was in munitions, from 212,000 to 947,000. These were the women, often young girls, who made weapons and filled shells in the huge government weapons factories like Woolwich Arsenal. There was also a big proportional increase in numbers of women in transport and nearly 3 million women worked in industry by 1918.

The only group of women workers whose numbers actually declined in the war was servants. All the other jobs offered greater freedom and perhaps interest and opportunity than being a servant.

Changing attitudes?

However, these changes did not come easily. There was lots of opposition to women working in manufacturing. Women soon showed that they could do the work, but many male workers resented them. The government had to promise the trade unions that men would have their jobs back when the war ended. In 1919 that happened very quickly. By 1920 fewer women were in employment than in 1914.

Source A

'Over and over again the foreman gave me wrong or incomplete instructions or altered them in such a way as to make me work more hours. None of the men spoke to me for a long time and would give me no help as to where to find things. My drawer was nailed up by the men, and oil was poured over everything in it through a crack one night.'

Dorothy Poole, who worked in an engineering factory during the war

Source B

'The work women are doing taxes the intelligence to a high degree. Yet the work turned out has reached a high pitch of excellence.'

From the journal *The Engineer* (1915)

Source C

'There is no reason to feel sympathetic towards the young woman who has been earning "pin money" while the men have been fighting. Women who left domestic service to enter a factory are now required to return to their pots and pans.'

An article in the *Southampton Times* (1918)

Specimen question

How far did the First World War change the position of women? [12 marks]

Hint

Note that this is a 'how far?' question. This means that the answer will NOT be total change or total non-change: it will be part change, and you have to say how much. Start with the obvious: the enormous changes in women's work in the war, nearly 2 million more working women. Then look at the other side: did attitudes change? Were the changes lasting?

The Vote

The 1918 Representation of the People Act gave the vote to all men, all women over 30 and women over 21 who owned their house, or who were married to a house-owner. This meant that the young munitions workers, whose efforts had done so much to supply the materials for military victory, did not get the vote. Not until 1928 did women get the right to vote on the same basis as men.

Source A

'Some years ago I used the expression "Let women work out their own salvation." Well, Sir, they have worked it out during the war. How could we have carried on the war without them? Wherever we look we see them doing work which three years ago we should have regarded as "men's work".'

Former Prime Minister Asquith, speaking in 1917

Specimen question

Was it the suffragettes, the suffragists or their war effort which won the vote for women? [14 marks]

Hint

This is a high-scoring question to which there is no single 'correct' answer. You must deal with the three explanations offered – suffragettes, suffragists and women's war effort and end each section with an evaluation of their importance. You could put them in your own order, ending with your own choice for the key factor. Source A pushes you towards giving credit to the war effort, but the pre-war activities of both groups set up the situation.

Check

That you know what happened to women after the war as well as during it.

Preview

What you need to know:

- In what ways the government controlled people's lives in the Second World War

- Why evacuation was carried out, who was evacuated and what was the impact of evacuation

- How conscription in the Second World War differed from the First, and how the war changed women's lives

- How much the government controlled information during the war

- Why rationing was introduced and how successful it was

- What the Blitz was and how far it affected the morale of the British people

- What the Beveridge Report proposed, and what kind of Welfare State was set up by the Labour Government after the war

Government control

In the Second World War the government tried to put into practice the lessons of the First World War (*see* Chapters 1 and 5). One of these was to move quickly to take control over many aspects of people's lives. They could see that victory in a modern war would only come if civilians as well as soldiers were organised for war – 'total war'. Civilians had to be protected, but they also had to serve the war effort and this included women as well as men. In this, Britain was far more successful than Germany which did not introduce 'total war' until late in the war.

Evacuation

In the First World War, 1413 civilians had been killed in air raids. By 1939 aeroplanes were much bigger and carried far heavier bombs. Government planners expected huge casualties as soon as war started – perhaps 600,000 in the first few days. Plans were made to evacuate all vulnerable people and within a few days a third of the British people had moved home.

The evacuation of 1.5 million people took place without a casualty. The meeting of city and country people was not so trouble-free.

Source A

Numbers and types of people evacuated

Schoolchildren	827,000
Mothers with young children	524,000
Expectant mothers	13,000
Blind and disabled people	7,000
Teachers and helpers	103,000

About 2 million made their own arrangements, many going to Canada and the USA.

Source B

'They are all filthy, the smell of the room is terrible, they refuse all food except tea and bread and the children have made puddles on the floor.'

Moya Woodside, describing evacuees from Belfast in 1939

Source C

'I think all London teachers resented the very wrong assumption made by many villagers that every child from London must have come from a slum, that they'd been neglected by their parents and that they were dirty.'

Stanley Reed, a London teacher, in a BBC film made in 1989

Source D

'My son and I were never homesick, we were too happy enjoying the beautiful Dorset scenery.'

A London evacuee mother, quoted in a book published in 1989

Specimen questions

1. Use Source A to describe evacuation and why it was carried out. **[6 marks]**

2. Describe the impact of evacuation on those who took part. **[7 marks]**

Hint

In question 1, explain why these people, not working adults, were evacuated, where they were evacuated from and where they were sent.

Hint

In question 2 you should make the point that it is hard to generalise from 1.5 million personal stories. You should use the sources and your own knowledge, but explain that sometimes they contradict each other, as Sources B and D do, for example.

By Christmas 1939, 60 per cent of evacuees had gone home, although some were evacuated again when the Blitz started in the winter of 1940.

Check

That you understand why evacuation was thought to be necessary.

Conscription

Conscription was introduced in April 1939, five months before the war even began. All men aged 18–40 had to fight or to work in certain important 'reserved occupations', such as coal mining.

A shortage of workers developed, as in 1916, because so many men were in the armed forces. This time the government did not hesitate: all women aged over twenty were conscripted. Britain was the only country to conscript women in this way. Eight times more women took on jobs in the Second World War than the First, and with far less opposition.

Many men and women worked very long hours – 80 or 90 hours a week was not uncommon.

Source A

These women pilots delivered planes, but never flew them in combat

Source B

'British women officers often give orders to the men. The men obey smartly and know it is no shame, for British women have proved themselves in this war. They have stuck to their posts near burning ammunition dumps, delivered messages on foot after their motorcycles have been blasted from under them. They have pulled aviators from burning planes. So when you see a girl in uniform with a bit of ribbon on her tunic, remember she didn't get it for knitting more socks than anyone else in Ipswich.'

Extract from a leaflet given to US soldiers sent to Britain in 1944.

Specimen question

In what ways was the experience of women in the Second World War different from the First? [9 marks]

Check

That you realise that both men and women were conscripted.

Information

The government controlled most kinds of information but did not use this control in the same way as the Nazis did in Germany.

- **Newspapers**
  The press was firmly censored. Bad news was reported, however, although often with a morale-boosting message.

- **Radio**
  The BBC was not censored by the government, but it did censor itself. Its clear, accurate news won the BBC 25 million listeners and a lasting reputation.

- **Collecting information**
  Civilian morale was vitally important in the war – if workers in the factories gave up, the war effort would collapse. The government set up 'Mass Observation' to collect information on what ordinary people were thinking.

- **Propaganda**
  Government wartime propaganda gave out information (*see* Sources A and B on page 125). It also tried to boost morale.

Source A

YOUR TALK
MAY KILL YOUR COMRADES

A wartime warning poster

Source B

TAKE THEM BACK!
TAKE THEM BACK!
TAKE THEM BACK!..

DON'T do it,
mother—

LEAVE THE CHILDREN
WHERE THEY ARE

ISSUED BY THE MINISTRY OF HEALTH

A government poster about evacuation

Specimen question

Use Sources A and B to describe the aims of government propaganda in the Second World War. [10 marks]

Check

That you recognise the different things that British wartime propaganda set out to do.

Model answer

The British government used propaganda in different ways in the Second World War. They made sure that a positive image of British success was put out, although they realised that if the message was too obviously biased no one would believe it. In this they were more successful than Nazi propaganda, which few people in Germany believed by 1940. The British government realised that no one was so stupid as to believe that everything was going well all the time, so bad news was announced as well as good. Of course, victories were proclaimed and the leadership of Winston Churchill was always praised.

Another purpose of government propaganda was simply to get people to do what the government wanted them to do. Source B is telling the public that evacuation was important and that children should not be brought home. (At the time, autumn 1939, lots of mothers were bringing their children home as the expected fierce bombing campaign had not happened.)

Source A is another kind of warning: telling people not to talk about things which enemy spies could hear and pass on. It is a powerfully designed poster, although it is doubtful if Britain was really so full of spies that ordinary conversations would be passed on.

British government propaganda in the Second World War was well thought out, on the whole, and quite effective.

Rationing

Britain does not produce enough food to feed everyone; lots has to be imported. As in the First World War, the German U-boat campaign was very effective in sinking large numbers of British ships. Food was soon in short supply. The government realised that a strict and fair system of rationing was needed, or else food prices would rise and ordinary people would go hungry.

Notes

- Everyone had to carry a ration book and food could only be bought if you had a coupon as well as the money. This meant that however rich you were, you could only buy the same amount of scarce foods as poorer people.
- Wages were good and food was kept cheap, so poorer people ate better in the war than in peacetime. Many were healthier in 1945 than in 1939.
- The government issued recipes to help people make the most of the ingredients available.
- There was always more food in country areas.
- Large families found it easier to manage on the rations than small families.
- Everyone was encouraged to grow their own food, with the slogan 'Dig for Victory'. Parks and golf courses were dug up for market gardens.
- Some items, for example tropical fruit such as oranges and bananas, disappeared until the war was over. So did luxuries like chocolate.
- Clothes were rationed, too. The choice was limited but the quality good.

There was a flourishing 'black market': goods sold illegally for cash.

Specimen question

Why was a food-rationing system needed and how effective was it?   [12 marks]

Check

That you can explain why rationing was necessary for Britain to win the war.

The Blitz

The Blitz was the bombing of British towns and cities. London was bombed on 7 September 1940: 19,000 tons of bombs were dropped, 430 people killed. There was a raid on London every night for the next 76 nights and then many more nights until June 1941. Smaller cities suffered too, sometimes sustaining a greater proportion of casualties. On 14 November 1940 Coventry was bombed: a third of its houses were destroyed, 554 people killed and 100 acres of the city centre flattened. After a raid on Clydebank, Scotland, only seven of the 2000 houses in the town were inhabitable.

Protection

- **Blackout**
  Every house had to black out all light. Street lights were dimmed and car lights hooded. This was to avoid giving clues to German bombers as to where towns or cities were.

- **Anderson shelters**
  Named after the Home Secretary Sir John Anderson, these consisted of curved sheets of metal. You bolted the sheets together, sank them a metre into the ground and put half a metre of earth on top. About 2 million were given out, but the shelters were quite small and only usable if you had a garden.

Source

Meat	1 shilling to two shillings and a pennyworth		Tea	2–4 oz	
Bacon	4–8 oz		Sugar	8–16 oz + 2 lbs for jam-making	
Cheese	1–8 oz		Sweets	3–4 oz (including chocolate)	
Fat	1–8 oz		Dried milk	1 tin	
Eggs	1–2		Dried eggs	8th of a packet	

- **Morrison shelters**
  Herbert Morrison was a later Home Secretary. This type of shelter was a big sheet of steel which you could get underneath.

- **Air Raid Protection (ARP)**
  ARP wardens were appointed to ensure the blackout was total and to help people into safe shelters.

- **Trekkers**
  Some people got out of the cities into the surrounding countryside every night. They were called trekkers and slept in ditches or barns until the morning.

- **Tube stations**
  At first the government refused to let people use the London tube stations as shelters as they were afraid people would go down and never come out. Only after Londoners forced their way into stations did the government allow people to shelter in them.

Source A

After the raid on Coventry, 14 November 1940

Source B

'By 4 p.m. all the platform and passage space of the underground station is staked out, chiefly with blankets folded in long strips against the wall – for the trains are still running and the platforms are in use. One child or woman guards the places and when evening comes the rest of the family crowd in.'

Tom Harrisson, *Living Through The Blitz* (1990)

Specimen questions

1   In what ways did the British people try to protect themselves against air raids?
    [6 marks]

2   What can you tell from the sources about the Blitz on Britain?   **[5 marks]**

Morale

The air raids did not have the impact people expected. Government planners expected huge casualties, including the use of poison gas. In fact 60,000 civilians died in air raids. This was many more than in the First World War, but nothing like the hundreds of thousands experts had predicted. Far more serious were incendiary bombs, which caused huge fires and destroyed homes, warehouses and factories. By May 1941 there were 1.4 million homeless Londoners.

The purpose of the Blitz was only partly to destroy factories and weapons. The Nazis also intended to break the morale of the British people so that they would lose the will to fight or to go to work. Government propaganda tried to give the impression that the 'Blitz spirit' was keeping life carrying on as normal.

Source A

'East London paused yesterday to lick its wounds after what had been planned as a night of terror. But it carried on.'

Daily Herald newspaper, September 1940

Source B

'More open than usual'

Sign on a shop

'Our windows are gone but our spirits are good – come in and try them.'

Sign on a pub

Source C

'There was very little absenteeism caused by the raids. This was partly because we all felt the raids gave an added importance to our work but more because we knew that if we didn't turn up our mates would be worrying. You would see men staggering at their work from lack of sleep, snatching a ten minute doze in the canteen over their food and still, when knocking off time came, going off with a cheerful "See yer in the morning, boys!"'

A man who worked in a Bristol aircraft factory during the war

Source D

'There were more open signs of hysteria observed in one evening than during the whole of the last two months. Women were seen to cry, to scream, to tremble all over, to faint in the street, to attack firemen, and so on.'

Report on Coventry after the big raid of November 1940

Source E

'Press reports of life going on normally in the East End [of London] are grotesque. There was no bread, no milk, no gas, no telephones. There was every excuse for people to be distressed. There was no understanding in the huge buildings of central London for the tiny crumbled streets of densely-massed population.'

Report on London, September 1940

Specimen question

1 'The "Blitz spirit" saw Britain through the hardships of the war.' Use the sources and your own knowledge to comment on the accuracy of this statement.

[12 marks]

Hint

Read through each of Sources A, B, C, D and E. Decide whether each one is evidence of a 'Blitz Spirit' or not, or is only propaganda.

Best answers will point out the evidence that there was a Blitz spirit, then list the evidence against, then come to a personal conclusion.

Check

That you understand why it was so important to keep the morale of the British people high.

The Welfare State

Even in the middle of the Second World War plans were made for a better Britain afterwards. There were several reasons for this:

- The war had thrown the British people together as never before. People met as evacuees and hosts, on trains and ships, in air-raid shelters. People talked to each other. Better-off Britons learned how poor and disadvantaged some people were.
- Efforts were made to make this a 'people's war', in which everyone was fairly treated. Many people wanted this attitude to continue after the war.
- There had been terrible poverty and unemployment in the 1930s, which became known as 'the wasted decade'. There was a determination to avoid such waste again.
- It was clear that Britain would need rebuilding after the war. What was to be the basis for post-war Britain? The British people needed a goal to fight for, to endure the hardships, shortages and fatigue.

The Beveridge Report 1942

In 1942 Sir William Beveridge wrote a report identifying 'Five Giants' blocking the road to happiness for all (*see* diagram).

Want
Poverty, caused by lack of earnings

Disease
Having to pay out for health care: doctor, hospital, etc.

Squalor
Bad housing

FIVE GIANTS

Ignorance
Poor education

Idleness
Unemployment

Source

A David Low cartoon published in the
Daily Express 1942

Implementing the Beveridge Report timeline

1946 National Insurance: every working person paid National Insurance out of their wages. In return, the state paid you when you couldn't earn for any reason, such as illness, old age, pregnancy or unemployment.

1948 National Assistance: this was additional support for anyone who was in financial difficulties.

1948 National Health Service: free health care for all. This included doctor's visits, dentistry, medicines, hospital care, glasses.

Specimen questions

1 The Beveridge Report was a boring read, but it sold 635,000 copies. Explain why it was so popular. [7 marks]

2 How does the cartoonist show his opinion of the Beveridge Report? [5 marks]

Specimen question

In what ways did the welfare measures introduced by the Labour government after the war put an end to Beveridge's 'Five Giants'? [10 marks]

Model answer

There are lots of clues which tell us that the cartoonist, Low, approved of the Beveridge Report. The bus is the 'social bus', containing the British people. Its destination is 'civilisation'. It is on a muddy, ruined road at present, but the 'Beveridge Way' (Lord Beveridge is holding the road sign) is clear and clean. Finally, the caption calls the turn the bus has to make to go down 'Beveridge Way', the 'right turn'.

Hint

List the 'Five Giants', then put the Labour government's actions alongside them. Which deals with which giant? Are they all dealt with?

Check

That you understand why the British people wanted these reforms when the war was over.

The Labour Government 1945–51

Although Winston Churchill, the Conservative leader, had been an immensely popular wartime Prime Minister, the General Election of 1945 brought a Labour landslide. One reason for this was their promise to put the Beveridge Report into action.

Index